CLASSROOM DATA TRACKING

Data-Tracking Tools at Your Fingertips!

Grade 4

Carson-Dellosa Publishing, LLC
PO Box 35665
Greensboro, NC 27425 USA
carsondellosa.com

978-1-4838-3442-9
01-158161151

Table of Contents

What Is Classroom Data Tracking?

Being able to prove student growth is more important than ever, making classroom data tracking essential in today's classroom. Data tracking is capturing student learning through both formative and summative assessments and displaying the results. Further assessment of the results can then become an active part of teaching, planning, and remediation. Because teachers are accountable to families and administrators, and time is always at a premium in the classroom, using a simple yet comprehensive data-tracking system is a must.

This book will help make this important data-collection task manageable. The data-tracking tools—charts, rubrics, logs, checklists, inventories, etc.—are easy to use and modifiable to fit any classroom. The tools will help you collect quantitative and qualitative information on each student's level of mastery in any part of your curriculum. Having specific details at your fingertips will aid in setting goals with students, keeping families informed, updating administrators, and displaying progress at student conferences.

An important component of good classroom data tracking is involving students in their own progress so that they can take ownership of their learning. Statistics prove that when students monitor their own learning and track their own growth, they are more highly motivated and perform better. In addition, a good data-tracking system presents avenues for celebrating student successes. Such opportunities are presented here, whether with an "I've done it!" check box or a rating score, and serve to create the intrinsic motivation we all want to see in students.

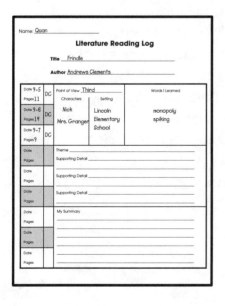 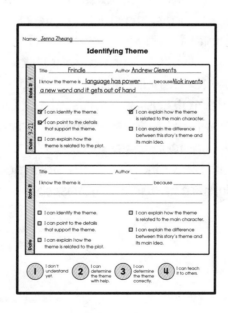 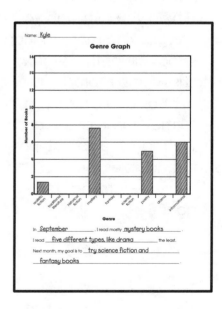

Completed data-tracking sheets for literature and theme

Why Should I Use Data Tracking?

Teachers are busy and do not need new tasks, but data tracking is a must because in today's data-driven classroom, information is crucial. Fortunately, classroom data tracking can be an at-your-disposal, invaluable tool in many ways:

- Data tracking creates a growth mindset. It shifts focus from a pass/fail mentality to one of showing growth over time.
- It allows you to see any gaps in concepts that need reteaching so that you can easily create focused remediation groups.
- It allows for more targeted lesson planning for the upcoming weeks. Pre-assessments can help you justify spending little to no time on skills that students have already mastered or more time on skills where students lack the expected baseline knowledge. Post-assessments can also help you determine whether students need more time or, if not, what topics you should address next.
- It provides you with daily information and allows you to give students feedback and guidance more regularly.
- It involves students with tracking their own data so that they can easily see their own progress.
- It gives students a sense of pride and ownership over their learning.
- It helps create data portfolios that are useful tools for families, administrators, and student conferences.

Data Tracking in Your Classroom

As standards become more rigorous, data tracking is becoming a necessary part of an already full daily classroom routine. The pages in this book are intended as tools that will help you manage your classroom data and create a customized system to make data tracking more manageable. This book is designed to allow you to choose the reproducibles that work specifically for you and your students. You may even choose to use some reproducibles only for certain groups of students instead of the entire class. This book also allows you to integrate assessments into your current routines by using informal observations and other formative assessments instead of interrupting the flow with traditional tests. If possible, try to involve students in tracking their own data by using reproducibles, graphs, and sample work to create and manage their own portfolios (for more detailed data-tracking management tips, see Managing Data Tracking on pages 8–9).

How to Use This Book

This book includes four main types of pages. Refer to the following sample pages and descriptions to help you get the most out of this resource.

Each anchor and domain section begins with a learning crosswalk. Use the crosswalk to help you better understand what students should know from the previous year and what they will need to know for the next year to better guide your plans for teaching, assessment, and remediation.

A concepts checklist follows the crosswalk for each anchor and domain. Use the checklist to track which concepts you have taught and when. Write the standard code (such as OA.A.1) in the top-left box and describe the concept in the large space. Use some or all of the boxes to the right to list the dates that you taught, tested, and retaught the concept. Make multiple copies as needed.

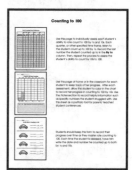

An explanation page precedes each set of three reproducibles. Use this page to learn about the intended use for each reproducible, to find additional suggestions for use, and to see an example of the reproducible in use.

The type of reproducibles included for each concept will vary according to the types of reproducibles that are most useful for assessing that concept. Reproducibles may include whole-class recording sheets, conference sheets, open-ended assessment pages, or pages where students take charge of their own goals and learning. Use the explanation page before each set to better understand how to use each page.

In addition, use the Standards Assessed chart on page 10 to plan for and keep track of the standards and related assessments for a single subject at a glance. Simply record all of the standards for the subject, the dates taught, and any other brief notes you choose to record (assessment types, overall class proficiency, etc.).

Getting Started

You can start data tracking at any point in the school year. If you are new to data tracking, it may be helpful to start small with a single subject until you become more comfortable with the process. Use the following guidelines to help you start a data-tracking system in your classroom (for more detailed data-tracking management tips, see Managing Data Tracking on pages 8–9).

1. Choose the best format for your classroom.

You may choose to have a single binder to collect data or have individual student binders or folders (for more information, see Which Format Is Best? on page 7).

2. Add a cover page.

Because the data-tracking binder will play a starring role in your school year, design an attractive cover that will make the binder identifiable and enjoyable to use. If students are also creating binders or folders, have them add cover pages as well.

3. Organize the binder(s) into sections.

Decide what subjects and topics you will be assessing and use tabs or dividers to clearly divide and label them.

4. Choose a rating system.

Although you may use different systems depending on what and how you will be assessing, use a single rating system for the majority of assessments to create consistency, cohesiveness, and clarity.

Use the following guidelines to help you set a clear tone for the year if using student binders as well.

5. Compose guidelines or a "mission statement."

Guidelines or a short "mission statement" will let students know what is expected of them and make them accountable with their data tracking. If desired, have students keep copies at the beginning of their notebooks and have both students and family members sign them at the beginning of the school year.

6. Have students set long-term and short-term goals.

Long-term goals will give students targets to work toward. Short-term goals will give students attainable checkpoints along the way. It may also be helpful to give students standards checklists in student-friendly language and to have students keep written goals in their binders as reminders.

Other Suggestions

Here are some additional important elements to consider before beginning a data-tracking system:

- *How to recognize students for their successes throughout the year.* Consider ideas such as placing stars programmed with students' names on a Reaching for the Stars bulletin board, giving special rewards, or giving verbal recognition along with a unique class cheer.

- *How to include families in this endeavor.* It can be as simple as sending letters home at the beginning of the year, having student-led conferences using the data binders, or sharing goals with families so that students can work on their goals at home as well.

- *How to maintain student binders.* It may be helpful to provide students with rubrics at the beginning of the year, outlining the expectations for maintaining and assessing their binders periodically to make sure that they continue to include samples and keep the binders neat and organized.

- *How to store student binders.* Decide where to keep the binders—at students' desks or in a separate location. If keeping them in a separate location, you may need to set guidelines for when students can access and add to them.

Which Format Is Best?

Because classroom data-tracking systems need to last for an entire year, many teachers create and maintain them in three-ring binders because of their durability. However, you may choose to keep student work in folders if space is an issue or if students will be storing less information.

A Single Teacher Binder	A Teacher Binder and Student Binders
Pros • Convenient format means the information can always be with you. • You can store all of the information in one place.	**Pros** • Students can move sample work with them each year. • You can include more information because space is not limited. • You have less to do when preparing for conferences.
Cons • You have to gather student work when preparing for conferences. • Space is limited.	**Cons** • It can be time-consuming to work with numerous binders. • It can be challenging to assess class proficiency when sample work is in individual binders.

Managing Data Tracking

Managing the Teacher Binder

- Choose a durable two- or three-inch binder to store all of the important information for the whole year.

- Use the teacher binder as the one place to store the following important assessment-related tools and reproducibles:
  - a copy of the standards at the front of your binder for easy reference
  - copies of the resources and assessment tools for your grade, such as pacing guides, word lists, fluency tests, and reading level charts
  - master copies of assessments (You may also choose to store these separately for space reasons.)

- Consider separating the binder into two sections—overall class proficiency and individual student data. In the class proficiency section, keep information such as what standards you taught when, overall class scores, and student grouping information. Use the individual student section to store running records, baseline tests, remediation forms, and anecdotal notes.

- At the beginning of the school year, assign students numbers and use a set of numbered tabs to organize individual student data in a single place. Add a copy of student names and assigned numbers to the front of the individual data section.

Managing Student Binders

- Consider copying yearlong tracking sheets on card stock instead of copy paper for durability.

- Color code sections to make it easier for students to quickly find the correct pages. For example, copy all sight word pages on yellow paper.

- For younger students, have volunteers preassemble the binders. Include all of the tracking sheets for the year (even if you won't use some until later) to avoid having to add pages later.

- Provide students with several three-hole-punched page protectors for storing sample work, which is often not prepunched.

- Devote a short, designated time each week to allow students to add sample work to and organize their binders.

Tips and Tricks

Organize everything.
- Use file folders to create dividing tabs in a binder. Cut off the half of a file folder with the tab, three-hole punch it, and place it in your binder.
- Keep binders simple by using one pocket for each subject.

Save time.
- Use pens in different colors to make recording dates on a recording sheet simpler. Instead of writing the same date numerous times, simply write the date once in one color and record all of the data from that day using that color. If adding data from another date, repeat with a different color.
- Choose a standard proficiency scale and use it consistently throughout the binder. For example,

E, P, M (emerging, progressing, mastered)	NS, B, OL, A (not seen, beginning, on level, above)
✓-, ✓, ✓+	-, +, ++
a 0–4 rubric	your own unique system

Fit assessment into your day.
- Keep sheets of large labels (such as 2" x 4") on a clipboard. Carry the clipboard throughout the day and use the labels to record any informal observations about individual students. Record each student's name, the date, and your observation on a label. At the end of the day, simply place the label in the corresponding student's section.
- Use your weekly or monthly plan to copy the relevant whole-class progress charts and conference sheets ahead of time. Keep them on a clipboard so that they are at hand when observing students throughout the week or month.
- Focus on assessing or observing only three to five students per day.

Make the reproducibles work for your classroom.
- Add text before copying to create a unique assessment.
- Add, remove, or alter items such as write-on lines or date lines.
- Use a different scale than suggested (see the table above for ideas).
- Use pencil when recording on whole-class checklists so that it is simple to change marks as students progress.
- Use highlighters to draw attention to skills that need remediation, to an individual student's areas of need, or to create targeted small groups.
- Highlight or add stickers beside student goals on graphs and other tracking sheets to give students something visible to work toward.

Standards Assessed

Subject _____ **Quarter** _____

Standard/Topic	Date	Date	Date	Date	Notes

Operations and Algebraic Thinking
Standards Crosswalk

Third Grade

Represent and solve problems involving multiplication and division.

• Interpret products of whole numbers.

• Interpret whole-number quotients of whole numbers.

• Use multiplication and division within 100 to solve word problems.

• Determine the unknown whole number in a multiplication or division equation relating three whole numbers.

Understand properties of multiplication and the relationship between multiplication and division.

• Apply properties of operations as strategies to multiply and divide.

• Understand division as an unknown-factor problem.

Multiply and divide within 100.

• Fluently multiply and divide within 100.

• Memorize all products of two one-digit numbers.

Solve problems involving the four operations, and identify and explain patterns in arithmetic.

• Use the four operations to solve two-step word problems with a variable used to represent the unknown quantity.

• Use strategies to decide if an answer is reasonable.

• Identify arithmetic patterns and explain them using properties of operations.

Fifth Grade

Write and interpret numerical expressions.

• Form and solve expressions with parentheses, brackets, or braces.

• Write and interpret simple numerical expressions.

Analyze patterns and relationships.

• Use given rules to generate two numerical patterns.

• Form ordered pairs from numerical patterns, and graph the ordered pairs on a coordinate plane.

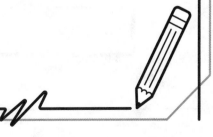

Operations and Algebraic Thinking
Concepts Checklist

Concept		Date(s) Taught				

Factors and Multiples

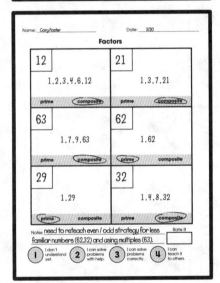

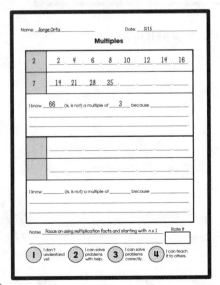

Use this page to help students keep track of their learning during a unit on factors and multiples. Before the unit, have students complete the first column by adding the date, and then circling, coloring, or highlighting the appropriate symbol for each I Can . . . statement. An *X* means *not yet*, a *?* means *maybe*, and a ✔ means *yes*. Then, after the unit, have students repeat these steps with the second column and answer the prompts at the bottom to assess their overall learning.

Assess students' understanding of factor pairs and prime and composite numbers. You may choose to assess only one topic at a time, or use the page as a comprehensive assessment. Program the top-left boxes with numbers. Students should list the factor pairs for each number and circle whether the number is prime or composite. You may also choose to have students orally justify why a number is prime or composite. If desired, divide the problems into two columns to allow for a pretest and posttest or a test and retest of the skills. Use the *Notes* section to record any observations.

Assess students' understanding of multiples. Program the two top-left boxes with numbers. Students should list the multiples for each number to the right. Program the first two spaces of the sentence, and have students circle *is* or *is not* and give an explanation to complete the sentence. Have students rate themselves using the scale at the bottom of the page. If desired, divide the page in half to allow for a pretest and posttest or a test and retest of the skills. Use the *Notes* section to record any observations.

Name: _____

Factors and Multiples

Skill	Date	Date
I can define *factor*.	✗ ? ✔	✗ ? ✔
I can find the factor pairs for any number 1–100.	✗ ? ✔	✗ ? ✔
I can define *prime*.	✗ ? ✔	✗ ? ✔
I can define *composite*.	✗ ? ✔	✗ ? ✔
I can identify if a number is prime or composite.	✗ ? ✔	✗ ? ✔
I can define *multiple*.	✗ ? ✔	✗ ? ✔
I can identify if any number 1–100 is a multiple of a number from 1–9.	✗ ? ✔	✗ ? ✔
I can explain how factors and multiples are related.	✗ ? ✔	✗ ? ✔

One thing I understand better now is

One thing I can still improve on is

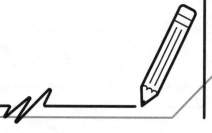

Factors

prime composite	prime composite
prime composite	prime composite
prime composite	prime composite

Notes _____

| 1 | I don't understand yet. | 2 | I can solve problems with help. | 3 | I can solve problems correctly. | 4 | I can teach it to others. |

Multiples

_____ , _____ , _____ , _____ , _____ , _____ , _____ , _____

_____ , _____ , _____ , _____ , _____ , _____ , _____ , _____

I know _____ (is, is not) a multiple of _____ because _____

_____

_____ .

_____ , _____ , _____ , _____ , _____ , _____ , _____ , _____

_____ , _____ , _____ , _____ , _____ , _____ , _____ , _____

I know _____ (is, is not) a multiple of _____ because _____

_____

_____ .

Notes _____

Rate It

 1 I don't understand yet.   **2** I can solve problems with help.   **3** I can solve problems correctly.   **4** I can teach it to others.

Word Problems

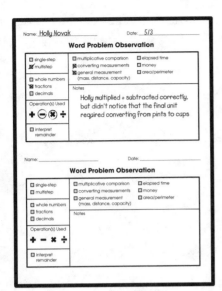

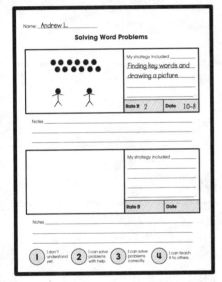

Use this page to assess students' proficiency with word problems throughout the year. Provide students with a word problem and check the appropriate boxes for that word problem (for example, this is a single-step problem dealing with whole numbers, division, and interpreting a remainder). If the problem more specifically deals with concepts such as measurement or elapsed time, check those boxes as well. Record observations and strategies observed in the *Notes* section. Store the word problem and student work with the observation sheet.

Understand a student's level of mastery in solving word problems with this page. Prompt students with a word problem they can solve in the blank area. Have students highlight key words on a copy of the word problem and attach it to the page. Then, have students complete the strategy prompt, rate themselves using the scale at the bottom of the page, and record the date. Use the *Notes* section to record observations about a student's understanding. Repeat throughout the year to collect a portfolio showing a student's progress. This page can also be used to assess a student's level of understanding of patterning.

Use this page to help students keep track of their understanding of word problems during the school year. Four times during the year, have students complete the first column by adding the date and then drawing the appropriate symbol for each I Can . . . statement using the key under the chart. Repeat several times to show progress through the year. After completing the last column, have students answer the prompts at the bottom to assess their overall learning. Or, have students complete it each time and date each observation.

Name: _____ Date: _____

Word Problem Observation

☐ single-step
☐ multistep

☐ whole numbers
☐ fractions
☐ decimals

Operation(s) Used

+ − ✖ ÷

☐ interpret remainder

☐ multiplicative comparison
☐ converting measurements
☐ general measurement (mass, distance, capacity)

☐ elapsed time
☐ money
☐ area/perimeter

Notes

Name: _____ Date: _____

Word Problem Observation

☐ single-step
☐ multistep

☐ whole numbers
☐ fractions
☐ decimals

Operation(s) Used

+ − ✖ ÷

☐ interpret remainder

☐ multiplicative comparison
☐ converting measurements
☐ general measurement (mass, distance, capacity)

☐ elapsed time
☐ money
☐ area/perimeter

Notes

Solving Word Problems

My strategy included _____

_____

_____

_____

_____ .

Rate It	Date

Notes _____

_____

_____

My strategy included _____

_____

_____

_____

_____ .

Rate It	Date

Notes _____

_____

_____

1 I don't understand yet.

2 I can solve problems with help.

3 I can solve problems correctly.

4 I can teach it to others.

Name: _____

Word Problems

Skill	Date	Date	Date	Date
I can choose the correct operation.				
I can identify key words.				
I can use a variety of strategies.				
I can solve multistep word problems.				
I can interpret remainders.				
I can solve word problems with fractions.				
I can solve word problems with decimals.				
I can solve word problems involving measurement (such as distance, weight, length, etc.).				
I can solve word problems involving elapsed time.				
I can solve word problems involving money.				
I can solve word problems involving area and perimeter.				

Ratings: ✗ = not yet   ? = maybe   ✓ = yes

One thing I understand well is

One thing I can improve on is

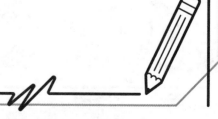

Number and Operations in Base Ten
Standards Crosswalk

Third Grade

Use place value understanding and properties of operations to perform multi-digit arithmetic.

• Round whole numbers to the nearest 10 or 100.
• Fluently add and subtract within 1,000.
• Multiply one-digit whole numbers by multiples of 10 from 10–90.

Fifth Grade

Understand the place value system.

• Understand that each place value is ten times larger than the place to the right, and one-tenth as large as the place to the left.
• Explain patterns in the number of zeros in a product when multiplying by a power of 10, and in the placement of the decimal point when a decimal is multiplied or divided by a power of 10.
• Use whole-number exponents to denote powers of 10.
• Read and write decimals to thousandths using base-ten numerals, words, and expanded form.
• Compare two decimals to the thousandths place using >, =, and <.
• Round decimals to any place.

Perform operations with multi-digit whole numbers and with decimals to hundredths.

• Fluently multiply multi-digit whole numbers.
• Find whole-number quotients by dividing up to four-digit dividends by two-digit divisors.
• Add, subtract, multiply, and divide decimals to the hundredths place.

Number and Operations in Base Ten
Concepts Checklist

Concept		Date(s) Taught				

Place Value

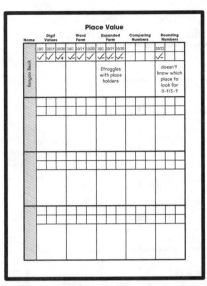

This page is useful for recording students' understanding of all place value concepts. Record student names in the left column. For each place value concept, you can record an assessment of a student's progress three times. Record the date at the top of each small box and the level of proficiency below using a system of your choosing, such as check marks or E/P/M. Use the large box below to record any observations.

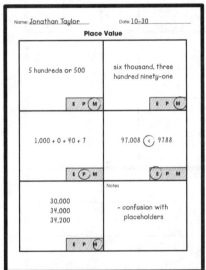

This page is ideal for assessing any or all place value concepts. You may choose to use all five boxes to assess the same concept or use each box to assess each of the five concepts. Provide students with a prompt, such as a number card, and then give them a place value task, such as *What is the value of the 5?* or *Write this number in expanded form.* Circle the E/P/M to assess the work in each box and use the *Notes* section to record any observations. Boxes are large enough to allow for more than one answer to be recorded, if desired.

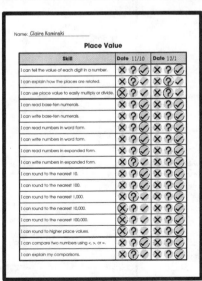

Use this page to help students keep track of their knowledge of place value concepts. Before the unit, have students complete the first column by adding the date and then circling, coloring, or highlighting the appropriate symbol for each I Can . . . statement. An *X* means *not yet*, a *?* means *maybe*, and a ✓ means *yes*. After the unit, have students repeat with the second column to assess how their learning changed.

Place Value

Name	Digit Values		Word Form		Expanded Form		Comparing Numbers		Rounding Numbers	

Name: _____   Date: _____

Place Value

E P M	E P M
E P M	E P M
	Notes
E P M	

Name: _____

Place Value

Skill	Date			Date		
I can tell the value of each digit in a number.	✗	?	✓	✗	?	✓
I can explain how the places are related.	✗	?	✓	✗	?	✓
I can use place value to easily multiply or divide.	✗	?	✓	✗	?	✓
I can read base-ten numerals.	✗	?	✓	✗	?	✓
I can write base-ten numerals.	✗	?	✓	✗	?	✓
I can read numbers in word form.	✗	?	✓	✗	?	✓
I can write numbers in word form.	✗	?	✓	✗	?	✓
I can read numbers in expanded form.	✗	?	✓	✗	?	✓
I can write numbers in expanded form.	✗	?	✓	✗	?	✓
I can round to the nearest 10.	✗	?	✓	✗	?	✓
I can round to the nearest 100.	✗	?	✓	✗	?	✓
I can round to the nearest 1,000.	✗	?	✓	✗	?	✓
I can round to the nearest 10,000.	✗	?	✓	✗	?	✓
I can round to the nearest 100,000.	✗	?	✓	✗	?	✓
I can round to higher place values.	✗	?	✓	✗	?	✓
I can compare two numbers using <, >, or =.	✗	?	✓	✗	?	✓
I can explain my comparisons.	✗	?	✓	✗	?	✓

Multiplication and Division

Use this page to track the class's overall proficiency with each type of multiplication and division and easily identify any need for remediation. Record each student's name in the left column. As you teach and assess each skill, record individual student proficiencies in the chart with a scale of your choosing. Use a pencil to allow for changing proficiencies as students complete remediation.

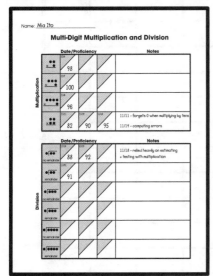

This page is useful for recording more detailed information about each student's proficiency with multiplication and division. As you assess students on each type of multiplication and division, record the date of assessment and the percentage correct. Use the far-right column to record any observations. Though up to three assessments can be recorded for each type, you may not need to use them all if a student has mastered the skill quickly.

This page is ideal for assessing any or all multiplication and division concepts. You may choose to use all six boxes to assess the same type of problem or use each box to assess a variety of problem types. Have students record the date in each of the top-left boxes if assessing over time. If assessing at a single time, students should only record the date once. Provide students with a multiplication or division problem, and have students copy and solve the problem in the large blank space. Then, have students use the 1–4 scale at the bottom to self-assess each problem.

Multi-Digit Multiplication and Division

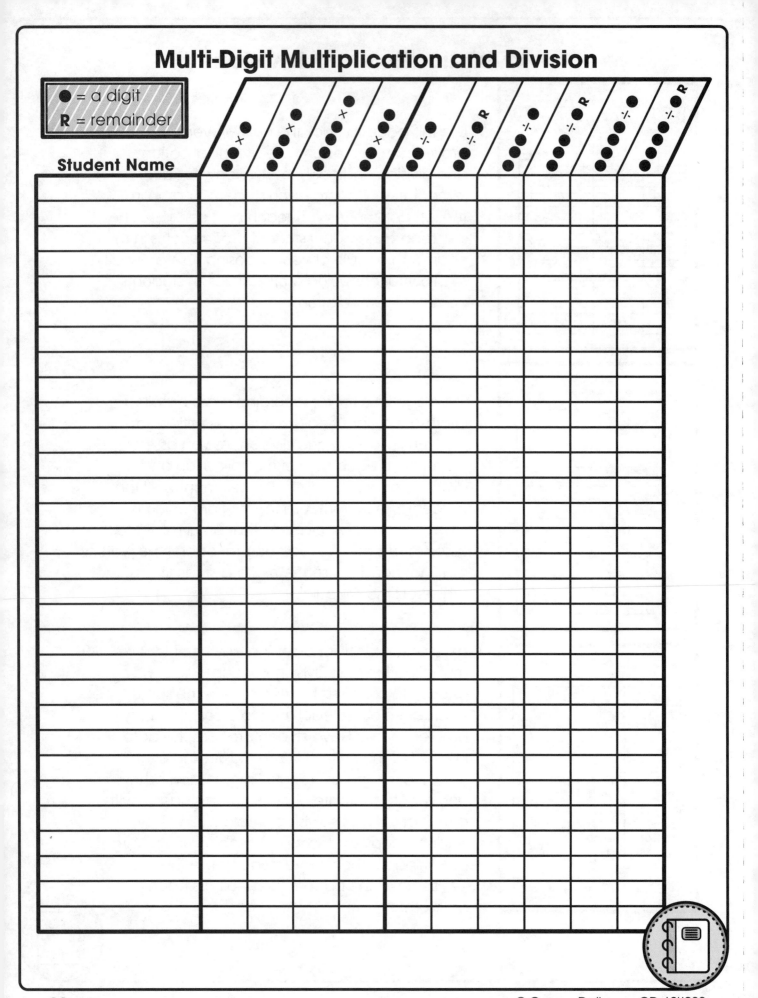

Multi-Digit Multiplication and Division

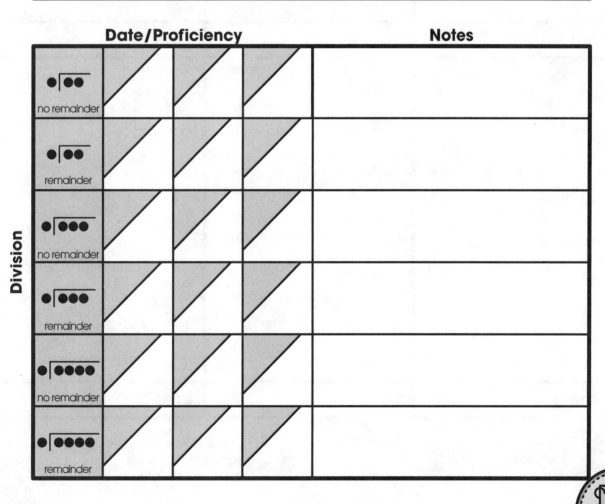

Multi-Digit Operations

Rate It	**Rate It**	**Rate It**
Rate It	**Rate It**	**Rate It**

 I don't understand yet.　　 I can solve problems with help.　　 I can solve problems correctly.　　 I can teach it to others.

Number and Operations—Fractions
Standards Crosswalk

Third Grade

Develop understanding of fractions as numbers.

• Recognize fractions as equal parts of a whole.
• Understand the significance of numerators and denominators.
• Represent a fraction on a number line from 0 to 1.
• Draw and divide a number line into equal parts in order to represent a fraction.
• Recognize and form simple equivalent fractions.
• Express whole numbers as fractions.
• Compare fractions that have the same numerator or same denominator using >, =, and <.

Fifth Grade

Use equivalent fractions as a strategy to add and subtract fractions.

• Add and subtract fractions and mixed numbers with unlike denominators using equivalent fractions.
• Solve word problems by adding and subtracting fractions.

Apply and extend previous understandings of multiplication and division to multiply and divide fractions.

• Understand that a fraction is the division of the numerator by the denominator.
• Solve division word problems where the answer is a fraction or a mixed number.
• Multiply a fraction or a whole number by a fraction.
• Find the area of a rectangle with fractional side lengths.
• Understand how multiplying by fractions affects the size of the product.
• Divide unit fractions by whole numbers and whole numbers by unit fractions.

Number and Operations—Fractions
Concepts Checklist

Concept		Date(s) Taught			

Equivalent Fractions

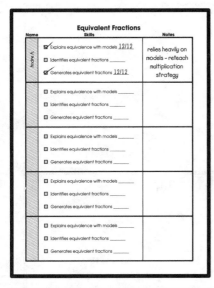

Use this page to track students' proficiency with equivalent fraction skills. Record student names in the first column. As each student demonstrates proficiency with a skill, check the box and record the date. Use the *Notes* section to record more detailed information and observations.

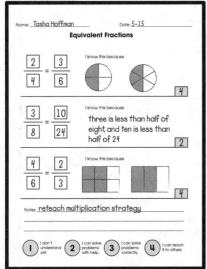

Use this page for individual assessment of equivalent fraction skills. Program one fraction and have students write an equivalent fraction, or program one fraction and the denominator of the second fraction and have students provide the numerator. Alternatively, complete both fractions and have students determine if the fractions are equivalent. Then, students should complete the reasoning section with models, number lines, etc. Have students rate their work in the small boxes on the right-hand side, using the 1–4 scale provided at the bottom of the page. Use the *Notes* section to record any observations.

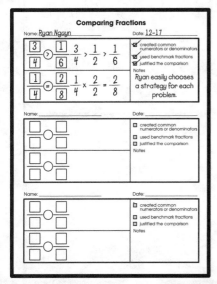

This page allows for individual assessment of comparing fractions. Program both fractions with numbers. Have each student write a comparative symbol in the circle, using the space to the right if needed to work out the solution. Then, check the boxes to show any strategies you observed and use the *Notes* section to record any observations.

Equivalent Fractions

Name	Skills	Notes
	☐ Explains equivalence with models _____ ☐ Identifies equivalent fractions _____ ☐ Generates equivalent fractions _____	
	☐ Explains equivalence with models _____ ☐ Identifies equivalent fractions _____ ☐ Generates equivalent fractions _____	
	☐ Explains equivalence with models _____ ☐ Identifies equivalent fractions _____ ☐ Generates equivalent fractions _____	
	☐ Explains equivalence with models _____ ☐ Identifies equivalent fractions _____ ☐ Generates equivalent fractions _____	
	☐ Explains equivalence with models _____ ☐ Identifies equivalent fractions _____ ☐ Generates equivalent fractions _____	

Name: _____   Date: _____

Equivalent Fractions

$$\frac{\square}{\square} = \frac{\square}{\square}$$

I know this because

$$\frac{\square}{\square} = \frac{\square}{\square}$$

I know this because

$$\frac{\square}{\square} = \frac{\square}{\square}$$

I know this because

Notes _____

_____

_____

1 I don't understand yet.   **2** I can solve problems with help.   **3** I can solve problems correctly.   **4** I can teach it to others.

Comparing Fractions

Name: _____   Date: _____

- [ ] created common numerators or denominators
- [ ] used benchmark fractions
- [ ] justified the comparison

Notes

Name: _____   Date: _____

- [ ] created common numerators or denominators
- [ ] used benchmark fractions
- [ ] justified the comparison

Notes

Name: _____   Date: _____

- [ ] created common numerators or denominators
- [ ] used benchmark fractions
- [ ] justified the comparison

Notes

Adding and Subtracting Fractions

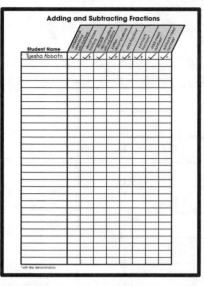

This page is useful for recording your class's proficiency with each part of adding and subtracting fractions. Record student names in the first column. Using either formal or informal assessments and a scale of your choosing, record individual student proficiencies for each skill.

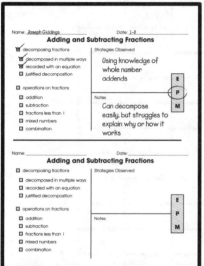

Use this page to record more detailed information about a formal or informal assessment. As you observe a student solve an addition or subtraction problem with fractions, place a check mark beside observed skills. Record any strategies you observe, and use the *Notes* section to record any additional observations. Then, circle *E*, *P*, or *M* to note whether the skills observed are emerging, progressing, or mastered. Store the student's work with the assessment.

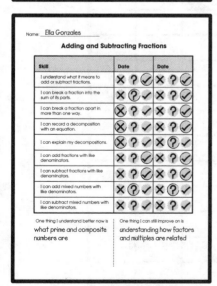

Use this page to help students keep track of their learning during a unit on adding and subtracting fractions. Before the unit, have students complete the first column by adding the date and then circling, coloring, or highlighting the appropriate symbol for each I Can . . . statement. An *X* means *not yet*, a *?* means *maybe*, and a ✓ means *yes*. Then, after the unit, have students repeat with the second column, and answer the prompts at the bottom to assess their overall learning.

Adding and Subtracting Fractions

Student Name	understands operations with fractions	decomposes fractions	records decompositions with equations	justifies decompositions	adds fractions*	subtracts fractions*	adds mixed numbers*	subtracts mixed numbers*

*with like denominators

Name: _____ Date: _____

Adding and Subtracting Fractions

☐ decomposing fractions

    ☐ decomposed in multiple ways

    ☐ recorded with an equation

    ☐ justified decomposition

☐ operations on fractions

    ☐ addition

    ☐ subtraction

    ☐ fractions less than 1

    ☐ mixed numbers

    ☐ combination

Strategies Observed

Notes

E
P
M

Name: _____ Date: _____

Adding and Subtracting Fractions

☐ decomposing fractions

    ☐ decomposed in multiple ways

    ☐ recorded with an equation

    ☐ justified decomposition

☐ operations on fractions

    ☐ addition

    ☐ subtraction

    ☐ fractions less than 1

    ☐ mixed numbers

    ☐ combination

Strategies Observed

Notes

E
P
M

Adding and Subtracting Fractions

Skill	Date	Date
I understand what it means to add or subtract fractions.	✗ ? ✓	✗ ? ✓
I can break a fraction into the sum of its parts.	✗ ? ✓	✗ ? ✓
I can break a fraction apart in more than one way.	✗ ? ✓	✗ ? ✓
I can record a decomposition with an equation.	✗ ? ✓	✗ ? ✓
I can explain my decompositions.	✗ ? ✓	✗ ? ✓
I can add fractions with like denominators.	✗ ? ✓	✗ ? ✓
I can subtract fractions with like denominators.	✗ ? ✓	✗ ? ✓
I can add mixed numbers with like denominators.	✗ ? ✓	✗ ? ✓
I can subtract mixed numbers with like denominators.	✗ ? ✓	✗ ? ✓

One thing I understand better now is

One thing I can still improve on is

Multiplying Fractions

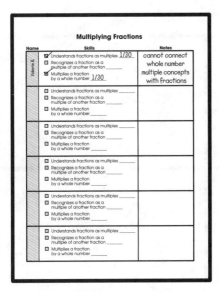

Use this page to track students' proficiency with multiplying fractions skills. Record student names in the first column. As each student demonstrates proficiency with a skill, check the box and record the date. Use the *Notes* section to record more detailed information and observations.

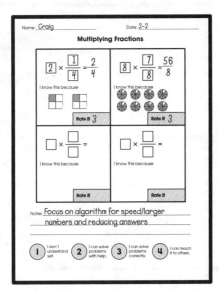

This page allows for individual assessment of multiplying fractions. Program the boxes with numbers to create multiplication sentences. Have students solve and complete the reasoning section with models, number lines, a written explanation, etc. Then, students should rate their work in the box at the bottom of each section, using the 1–4 scale provided at the bottom of the page. Use the *Notes* section to record any observations. If desired, split the page in half and use as a pretest and posttest or as a test and retest.

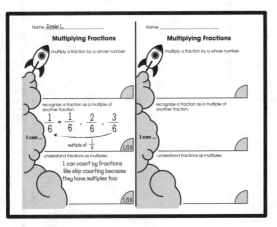

Students can take charge of their learning with this page. Once a student masters a skill, have her add the date to the bottom right section of that skill, use the blank area to write or draw proof of mastery, and color the section or you may choose to make this into a goal sheet for students struggling with these skills. Simply have students use the date space to write a goal date and use the blank area to list action items. Allow students to color each goal when it has been achieved.

Multiplying Fractions

Name	Skills	Notes
	☐ Understands fractions as multiples _____ ☐ Recognizes a fraction as a multiple of another fraction _____ ☐ Multiplies a fraction by a whole number _____	
	☐ Understands fractions as multiples _____ ☐ Recognizes a fraction as a multiple of another fraction _____ ☐ Multiplies a fraction by a whole number _____	
	☐ Understands fractions as multiples _____ ☐ Recognizes a fraction as a multiple of another fraction _____ ☐ Multiplies a fraction by a whole number _____	
	☐ Understands fractions as multiples _____ ☐ Recognizes a fraction as a multiple of another fraction _____ ☐ Multiplies a fraction by a whole number _____	
	☐ Understands fractions as multiples _____ ☐ Recognizes a fraction as a multiple of another fraction _____ ☐ Multiplies a fraction by a whole number _____	
	☐ Understands fractions as multiples _____ ☐ Recognizes a fraction as a multiple of another fraction _____ ☐ Multiplies a fraction by a whole number _____	

Multiplying Fractions

$$\square \times \frac{\square}{\square} =$$

I know this because

Rate It

$$\square \times \frac{\square}{\square} =$$

I know this because

Rate It

$$\square \times \frac{\square}{\square} =$$

I know this because

Rate It

$$\square \times \frac{\square}{\square} =$$

I know this because

Rate It

Notes _____

_____

_____

1 I don't understand yet.

2 I can solve problems with help.

3 I can solve problems correctly.

4 I can teach it to others.

Name: _____

Multiplying Fractions

multiply a fraction by a whole number.

recognize a fraction as a multiple of another fraction.

I can ...

understand fractions as multiples.

Name: _____

Multiplying Fractions

multiply a fraction by a whole number.

recognize a fraction as a multiple of another fraction.

I can ...

understand fractions as multiples.

Fractions and Decimals

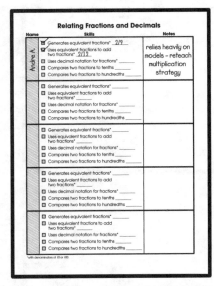

Use this page to track students' proficiency with understanding the relationship between fractions and decimals. Record student names in the first column. As each student demonstrates proficiency with a skill, check the box and record the date. Use the *Notes* section to record more detailed information and observations.

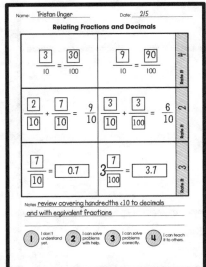

This page allows for individual assessment of relating fractions and decimals. In the top section, program either fraction and have students complete its equivalent. In the middle section, program both fractions and have students add. In the bottom section, program the fraction or decimal and have students complete the equivalent. Students should rate their work using the 1–4 scale provided at the bottom of the page. Use the *Notes* section to record observations. If desired, divide the page in half and use as a pretest and posttest or test and retest.

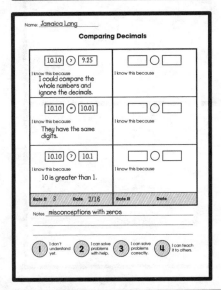

Use this page for individual assessment of comparing decimals. Program the boxes with decimals and have students complete the comparison. Or, program a complete comparison and challenge students to prove it right or wrong. Have students complete the reasoning section with models, a written explanation, etc. Students should date and rate their work using the 1–4 scale at the bottom of the page. Use the *Notes* section to record observations. If desired, divide the page in half and use as a pretest and posttest or test and retest.

Relating Fractions and Decimals

Name	Skills	Notes
	☐ Generates equivalent fractions* _____ ☐ Uses equivalent fractions to add two fractions* _____ ☐ Uses decimal notation for fractions* _____ ☐ Compares two fractions to tenths _____ ☐ Compares two fractions to hundredths _____	
	☐ Generates equivalent fractions* _____ ☐ Uses equivalent fractions to add two fractions* _____ ☐ Uses decimal notation for fractions* _____ ☐ Compares two fractions to tenths _____ ☐ Compares two fractions to hundredths _____	
	☐ Generates equivalent fractions* _____ ☐ Uses equivalent fractions to add two fractions* _____ ☐ Uses decimal notation for fractions* _____ ☐ Compares two fractions to tenths _____ ☐ Compares two fractions to hundredths _____	
	☐ Generates equivalent fractions* _____ ☐ Uses equivalent fractions to add two fractions* _____ ☐ Uses decimal notation for fractions* _____ ☐ Compares two fractions to tenths _____ ☐ Compares two fractions to hundredths _____	
	☐ Generates equivalent fractions* _____ ☐ Uses equivalent fractions to add two fractions* _____ ☐ Uses decimal notation for fractions* _____ ☐ Compares two fractions to tenths _____ ☐ Compares two fractions to hundredths _____	

*with denominators of 10 or 100

Relating Fractions and Decimals

$$\frac{\boxed{}}{10} = \frac{\boxed{}}{100}$$

$$\frac{\boxed{}}{10} = \frac{\boxed{}}{100}$$

Rate It

$$\frac{\boxed{}}{\boxed{}} + \frac{\boxed{}}{\boxed{}} =$$

$$\frac{\boxed{}}{\boxed{}} + \frac{\boxed{}}{\boxed{}} =$$

Rate It

$$\frac{\boxed{}}{\boxed{}} = \boxed{}$$

$$\frac{\boxed{}}{\boxed{}} = \boxed{}$$

Rate It

Notes _____

_____

_____

 1 I don't understand yet.

 2 I can solve problems with help.

 3 I can solve problems correctly.

4 I can teach it to others.

Name: _____

Comparing Decimals

I know this because

I know this because

I know this because

I know this because

I know this because

I know this because

| Rate It | Date | Rate It | Date |

Notes _____

_____

_____

1 I don't understand yet.   **2** I can solve problems with help.   **3** I can solve problems correctly.   **4** I can teach it to others.

Measurement and Data
Standards Crosswalk

Third Grade

Measure and estimate intervals of time, liquid volumes, and mass to solve problems.

- Tell and write time to the nearest minute, including measurement of time intervals.
- Solve word problems involving addition and subtraction of time intervals in minutes.
- Measure and estimate liquid volume and mass using grams, kilograms, and liters.
- Solve volume and mass word problems given in the same units.

Represent and interpret data.

- Draw scaled picture and bar graphs to represent several categories.
- Analyze graphs to solve one- and two-step problems.
- Measure lengths to halves and fourths of an inch.
- Show fractional measurement data by creating line plots.

Geometric measurement: understand area and relate it to multiplication and addition.

- Recognize area as an attribute of plane figures.
- Understand the concept of a square unit.
- Find area by counting unit squares and correctly laying square units side by side.
- Relate area to multiplication and addition in real world problems using tiling and area models.
- Find areas of rectilinear figures by dividing them into non-overlapping rectangles and adding the areas of the rectangles.

Geometric measurement: understand perimeter and distinguish between linear and area measures.

- Find perimeters of polygons.
- Use perimeter to find unknown side lengths.
- Exhibit rectangles with the same perimeter and different areas or vice versa.

Fifth Grade

Convert like measurement units within a given measurement system.

- Convert measurement units within a measurement system.

Represent and interpret data.

- Make a line plot displaying fractions.
- Solve problems involving fifth-grade fraction operations on line plot data.

Geometric measurement: understand volume and relate it to multiplication and to addition.

- Understand the concept of volume.
- Recognize one cubic unit of volume.
- Understand that volume is measured using cubic units to fill a solid figure.
- Measure volume using various units.
- Understand the formulas $V = l \times w \times h$ and $V = b \times h$ to find the volume of rectangular prisms.
- Find the volume of complex solid figures by finding the volumes of rectangular prisms within the figure and adding them together.

Measurement and Data Concepts Checklist

Concept		Date(s) Taught				

Measurement

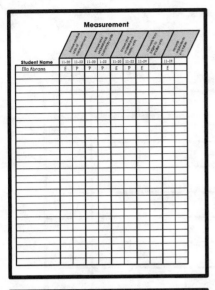

This page is useful for recording a student's understanding of all measurement concepts. Record student names in the left column. For each measurement concept, you can record an assessment of a student's progress twice, such as with a pretest and posttest or a test and retest. Record the date at the top of each column and the level of proficiency below using a system of your choosing, such as check marks or E/P/M.

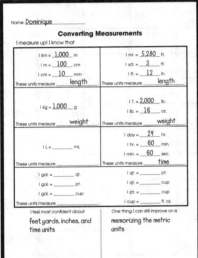

Students can take charge of their learning with this page. As students master a metric or customary unit, have them complete the section with the correct answers and color the section. When students have mastered all units, have them complete the prompts at the bottom of the page to assess their overall learning during the unit.

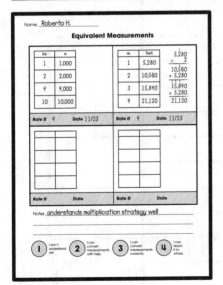

Use this page to assess converting measurements using tables. Write two related units at the top of each chart. Program the left column with measurements and have students complete the right column. Have students use the space to the right for working out their answers. Have students date and rate each problem at the bottom of the box using the 1–4 scale at the bottom of the page. Use the *Notes* section to record observations. If desired, divide the page in half to use as a pretest and posttest or test and retest. This page can also be used to assess patterning with numbers and function machines.

Measurement

Student Name	knows relative units of measurement	knows and understands customary units	knows and understands metric units	converts from larger to smaller units	records equivalents in a table

Name: _____

Converting Measurements

I measure up! I know that

I km = _____ m	I mi. = _____ ft.
I m = _____ cm	I yd. = _____ ft.
I cm = _____ mm	I ft. = _____ in.
These units measure _____.	These units measure _____.

I kg = _____ g	I T. = _____ lb.
	I lb. = _____ oz.
These units measure _____.	These units measure _____.

I L = _____ mL	I day = _____ hr.
	I hr. = _____ min.
	I min. = _____ sec.
These units measure _____.	These units measure _____.

I gal. = _____ qt.	I qt. = _____ pt.
I gal. = _____ pt.	I qt. = _____ cup
I gal. = _____ cup	I pt. = _____ cup
These units measure _____.	I cup = _____ fl. oz.

I feel most confident about

One thing I can still improve on is

Name: _____

Equivalent Measurements

Rate It   **Date**

Rate It   **Date**

Rate It   **Date**

Rate It   **Date**

Notes _____

_____

_____

 1 I don't understand yet.

 2 I can convert measurements with help.

 3 I can convert measurements correctly.

 4 I can teach it to others.

Graphing

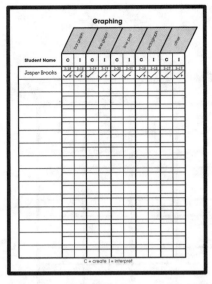

This page is useful for recording a student's understanding of all graphing concepts. Record student names in the left column. For each graphing concept, you can assess a student's ability to create that type of graph as well as interpret the data. Record the assessment date at the top of each column and the level of proficiency below using a system of your choosing, such as check marks or E/P/M.

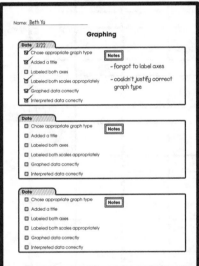

Use this page to record more detailed information about a student's formal or informal graphing assessments throughout the year. As you observe a student create or interpret a graph, place a check mark beside demonstrated skills. Use the *Notes* section to record any additional observations. If desired, mark through any skills you are not assessing at that time. Store the student's work with the assessment.

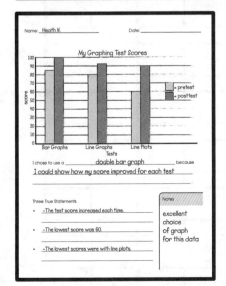

Provide students with this graphing assessment at the end of the unit. Provide students with a data set, such as their assessment scores from the unit. Students should create an appropriate graph using the data and use the graph to complete the prompts at the bottom of the page. Use the *Notes* section at the bottom right to record any observations. If desired, use with page 57 to assess the specific graphing tasks required by this assessment.

Graphing

Student Name	bar graph		line graph		line plot		pictograph		other	
	C	**I**	**C**	**I**	**C**	**I**	**C**	**I**	**C**	**I**

C = create I = interpret

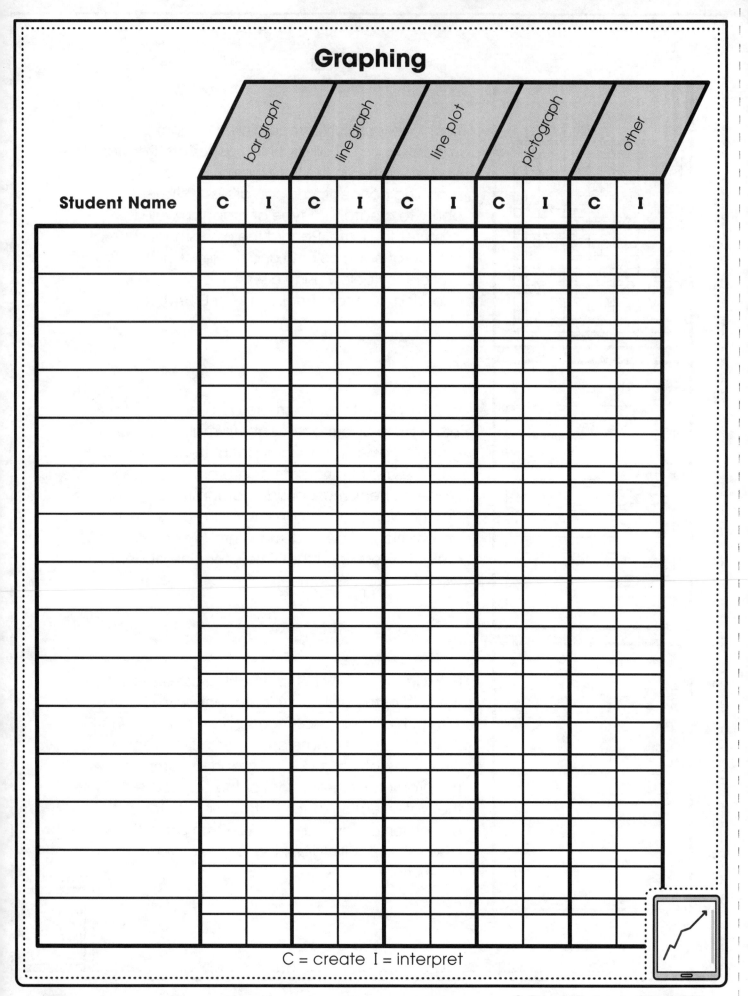

Name: _____

Graphing

Date ///////////

- ☐ Chose appropriate graph type
- ☐ Added a title
- ☐ Labeled both axes
- ☐ Labeled both scales appropriately
- ☐ Graphed data correctly
- ☐ Interpreted data correctly

Notes

Date ///////////

- ☐ Chose appropriate graph type
- ☐ Added a title
- ☐ Labeled both axes
- ☐ Labeled both scales appropriately
- ☐ Graphed data correctly
- ☐ Interpreted data correctly

Notes

Date ///////////

- ☐ Chose appropriate graph type
- ☐ Added a title
- ☐ Labeled both axes
- ☐ Labeled both scales appropriately
- ☐ Graphed data correctly
- ☐ Interpreted data correctly

Notes

Graphing

I chose to use a _____ because

_____

_____ .

Three True Statements

- _____

   _____

- _____

   _____

- _____

   _____

Notes

Angles

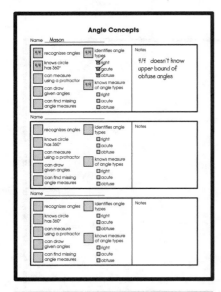

Use this page to track each student's mastery of angles and related concepts. As a student masters each concept, check or date it. Use the *Notes* section to record any observations. For clarity, date each observation if they are made on different dates.

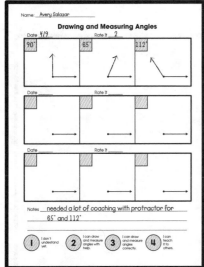

Use this page to assess a student's understanding of drawing angles and angle measurement. Write an angle measure in the top-left box in each section and have the student draw the matching angle. Draw a ray to complete each angle and have the student use a protractor to measure each angle and record the angle measure in the top-left box. Alternatively, challenge the student to draw a different angle type in each box. Date each row, or only date the top row if using all nine boxes at once. Have the student use the 1–4 scale at the bottom of the page to rate their work. Use the *Notes* section to record any observations.

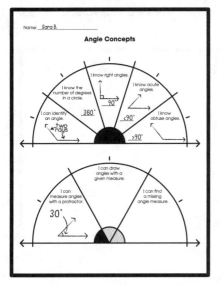

Students can celebrate their learning with this page. Once a student masters a skill, she should draw an example or complete the blank in each section to prove proficiency. Then, have her shade the small section at the bottom of each large section red, yellow, or green to indicate her comfort level with the skill. If desired, have students record the date of mastery for each skill outside of the semicircle.

Angle Concepts

Name _____

		Notes
☐ recognizes angles	☐ identifies angle types	
☐ knows circle has 360°	☐ right	
	☐ acute	
☐ can measure using a protractor	☐ obtuse	
	☐ knows measure of angle types	
☐ can draw given angles	☐ right	
☐ can find missing angle measures	☐ acute	
	☐ obtuse	

Name _____

		Notes
☐ recognizes angles	☐ identifies angle types	
☐ knows circle has 360°	☐ right	
	☐ acute	
☐ can measure using a protractor	☐ obtuse	
	☐ knows measure of angle types	
☐ can draw given angles	☐ right	
☐ can find missing angle measures	☐ acute	
	☐ obtuse	

Name _____

		Notes
☐ recognizes angles	☐ identifies angle types	
☐ knows circle has 360°	☐ right	
	☐ acute	
☐ can measure using a protractor	☐ obtuse	
	☐ knows measure of angle types	
☐ can draw given angles	☐ right	
☐ can find missing angle measures	☐ acute	
	☐ obtuse	

Drawing and Measuring Angles

Date _____   Rate It _____

Date _____   Rate It _____

Date _____   Rate It _____

Notes _____

_____

_____

1 I don't understand yet.

2 I can draw and measure angles with help.

3 I can draw and measure angles correctly.

4 I can teach it to others.

Angle Concepts

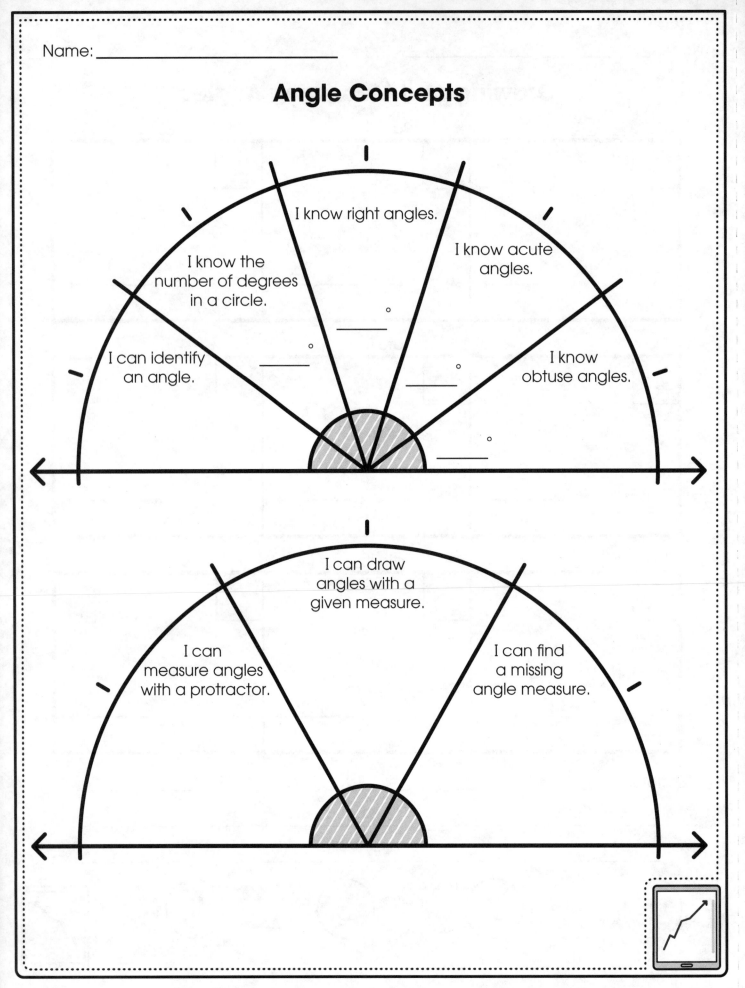

I know right angles.

I know the number of degrees in a circle.

I know acute angles.

I can identify an angle.

I know obtuse angles.

_____ °

_____ °

_____ °

_____ °

I can draw angles with a given measure.

I can measure angles with a protractor.

I can find a missing angle measure.

Geometry
Standards Crosswalk

Third Grade

Reason with shapes and their attributes.

• Understand that shapes in different categories may share attributes, and that the shared attributes can define a larger category.

• Recognize rhombuses, rectangles, and squares as examples of quadrilaterals, and draw examples of quadrilaterals that do not belong to any of these subcategories.

• Partition shapes into parts with equal areas.

• Express the area of each part of a partition as a unit fraction of the whole.

Fifth Grade

Graph points on the coordinate plane to solve real-world and mathematical problems.

• Understand a coordinate system and coordinates.

• Plot ordered pairs in the first quadrant of the coordinate plane.

• Use points to represent real-world problems and interpret the value of points in the context of the data they represent.

Classify two-dimensional figures into categories based on their properties.

• Recognize that all two-dimensional figures within a subcategory share the same attributes of the larger category.

• Classify two-dimensional figures in a hierarchy based on properties.

Geometry Concepts Checklist

Concept		Date(s) Taught				

Geometric Objects and Symmetry

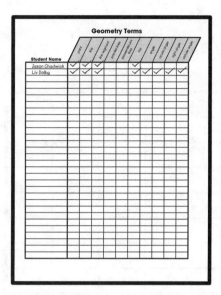

This page is useful for recording each student's proficiency with geometry terms. Record student names in the first column. Using either formal or informal assessments and a scale of your choosing, record individual student proficiencies for each geometry term.

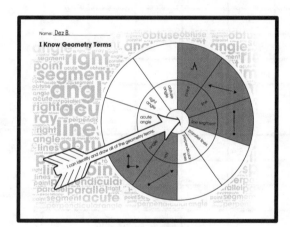

Students can celebrate their learning with this page. Once a student can recognize and draw a geometric term, he should draw an example of the term, write a definition, or do both in the blank section to prove understanding. If desired, have students record the date of mastery for each term as well. Then, have him shade the section. Once all sections have been shaded, he can color the arrow to celebrate that he knows all of the geometry terms.

This page is useful for recording each student's proficiency with symmetry. Using either formal or informal assessments and a scale of your choosing, record individual student proficiencies for each symmetry skill. Use the *Notes* column to record any observations.

Geometry Terms

Student Name	point	line	line segment	parallel lines	perpendicular lines	ray	angle	acute angle	right angle	obtuse angle

Name: _____

I Know Geometry Terms

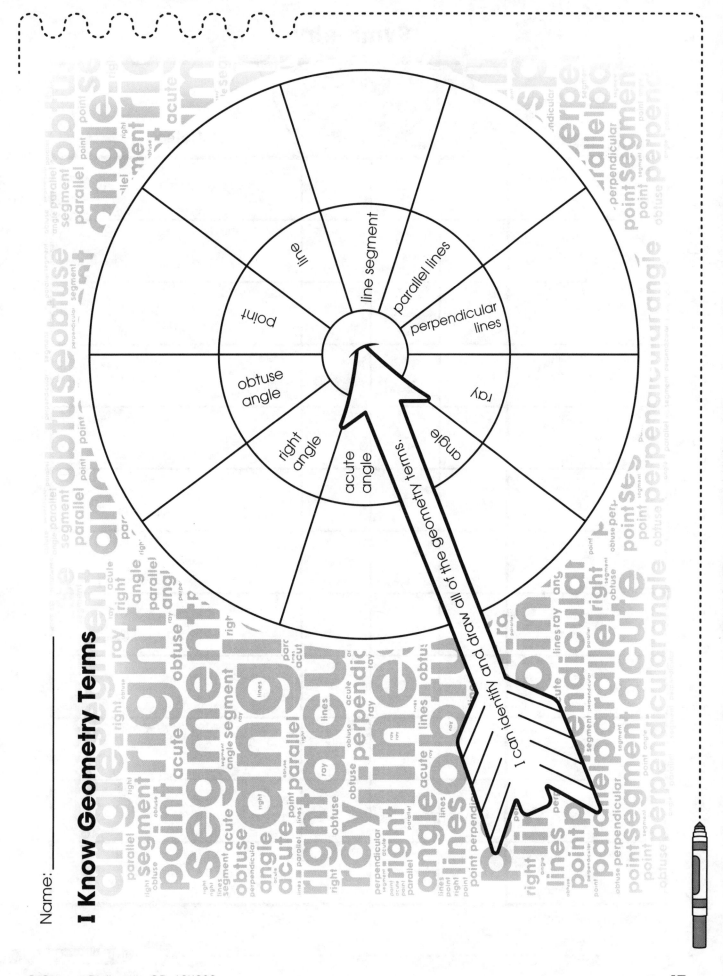

The wheel contains the following geometry terms: line, line segment, parallel lines, perpendicular lines, ray, angle, acute angle, right angle, obtuse angle, point

I can identify and draw all of the geometry terms.

Symmetry

Student Name	identify a line of symmetry	identify symmetric figures	draw lines of symmetry	Notes

*with like denominators

Reading: Literature
Standards Crosswalk

Third Grade

Key Ideas and Details

- Refer to text to ask and answer questions to demonstrate understanding.
- Recount stories, including fables, folktales, and myths from diverse cultures.
- Use key details to determine the central message, lesson, or moral in a text.
- Describe characters in a story and explain how their actions contribute to the sequence of events.

Craft and Structure

- Distinguish literal from nonliteral language when determining the meaning of words and phrases in a text.
- Refer to parts of stories, dramas, and poems when writing or speaking about a text, using terms such as *chapter*, *scene*, and *stanza*.
- Describe how each successive part of a story, drama, or poem builds on earlier sections.
- Distinguish their own points of view from those of the narrator or characters.

Integration of Knowledge and Ideas

- Explain how the illustrations support what is conveyed in the text.
- Compare and contrast the themes, settings, and plots of stories written by the same author about the same or similar characters.

Range of Reading and Level of Text Complexity

- By the end of the year, read and comprehend literature independently at the high end of the grades 2–3 text complexity band.

Fifth Grade

Key Ideas and Details

- Use quotes and evidence from a text to explain and draw inferences.
- Use specific details to determine the theme of a text, including character responses and reflections.
- Summarize a text.
- Compare and contrast two or more characters, settings, or events in a story or drama, drawing on specific details in the text.

Craft and Structure

- Determine the meaning of words and phrases in a text, including figurative language.
- Explain the connection between chapters, scenes, and stanzas as part of a text's structure.
- Describe how point of view affects descriptions of events.

Integration of Knowledge and Ideas

- Analyze how visual and multimedia elements contribute to the meaning, tone, or beauty of a text.
- Compare and contrast the approach to similar themes and topics in stories from the same genre.

Range of Reading and Level of Text Complexity

- By the end of the year, independently read and comprehend literature at the high end of the grades 4–5 text complexity band.

Reading: Literature Concepts Checklist

Concept		Date(s) Taught				

Reading Literature

Use this page as a take-home reading log for literature. Each student should use one page for a single book she reads at home. Each night, have her record the date and number of pages she read along the left side. A family member should initial to the right. Then, as the student progresses through the book, she should complete the right-hand side of the page with information about the book.

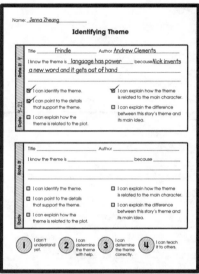

This page is useful for spotchecking students' understanding of theme throughout the year. Have the student date the left side and complete the prompts about a book they have recently read. Then, students should check off the skills they feel confident about and add a self-rating to the left side using the 1–4 scale at the bottom of the page.

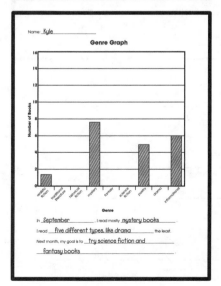

Provide this page to students each month or quarter. Have students use the graph to track how many books or texts they have read in each genre during that time. At the end of the month or quarter, have students complete the prompts at the bottom of the page. Use the graph during individual reading conferences to help students set individual reading goals.

Literature Reading Log

Title _____

Author _____

Date		Point of View _____		Words I Learned
Pages		Characters	Setting	
Date				
Pages				
Date				
Pages				

Theme _____

Supporting Detail _____
_____

Supporting Detail _____
_____

Supporting Detail _____
_____

My Summary
_____
_____
_____
_____
_____
_____
_____

Identifying Theme

Title _____ Author _____

I know the theme is _____ because _____

_____

_____

☐ I can identify the theme.

☐ I can point to the details that support the theme.

☐ I can explain how the theme is related to the plot.

☐ I can explain how the theme is related to the main character.

☐ I can explain the difference between this story's theme and its main idea.

Rate It

Date

Title _____ Author _____

I know the theme is _____ because _____

_____

_____

☐ I can identify the theme.

☐ I can point to the details that support the theme.

☐ I can explain how the theme is related to the plot.

☐ I can explain how the theme is related to the main character.

☐ I can explain the difference between this story's theme and its main idea.

Rate It

Date

 1 I don't understand yet.

 2 I can determine the theme with help.

 3 I can determine the theme correctly.

 4 I can teach it to others.

Name: _____

Genre Graph

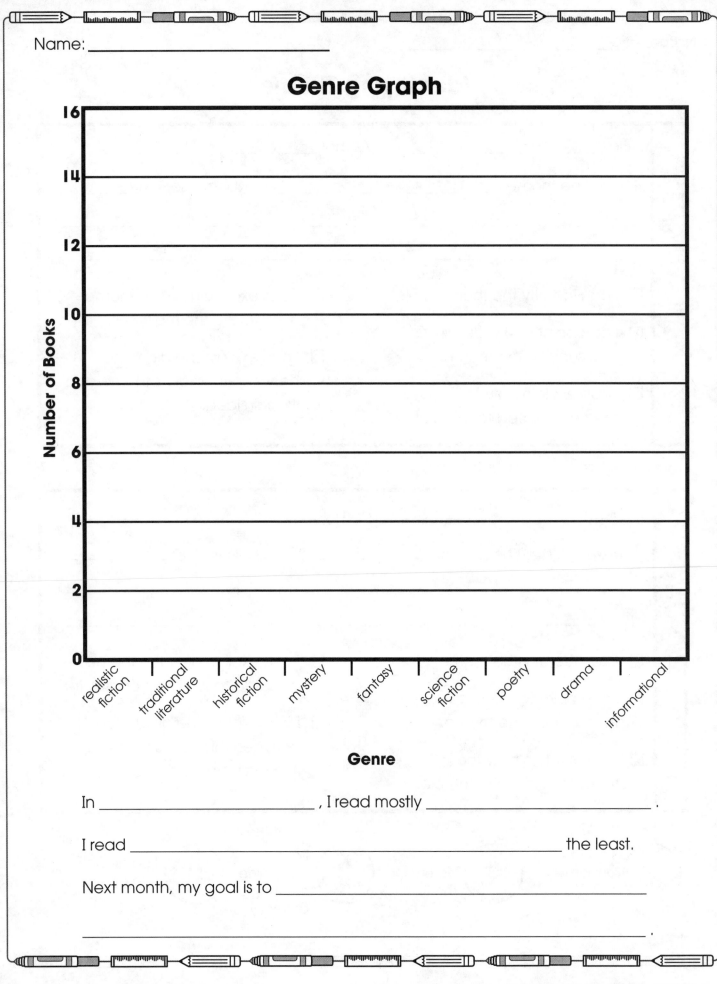

Number of Books

16
14
12
10
8
6
4
2
0

realistic fiction   traditional literature   historical fiction   mystery   fantasy   science fiction   poetry   drama   informational

Genre

In _____ , I read mostly _____ .

I read _____ the least.

Next month, my goal is to _____

_____ .

Story Elements

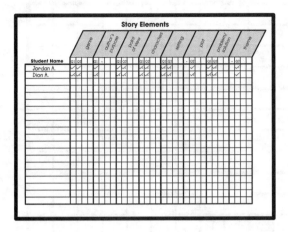

This page is useful for recording each student's understanding of all story element concepts. Record student names in the left column. For each concept, you can record an assessment of a student's progress four times throughout the year, such as quarterly. Record the date at the top of each column and the level of proficiency below using a system of your choosing, such as check marks or E/P/M.

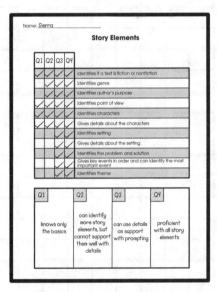

Use this page to record individual student proficiency with each story element concept throughout the year. Record the date of assessment or the quarter at the top of each column. For each skill, check proficiency with formal or informal assessment and check each appropriate box. Use the boxes at the bottom to record any notes or observations on each of the four dates. Write the date of the observation in the top-left corner of each box.

Provide this page to students to use as a book report form. After a student has completed a fiction book, he should fill out the prompts about that story. Use the page to gauge students' understanding of story elements. If desired, store each report with a student's assessment data, such as page 77.

Story Elements

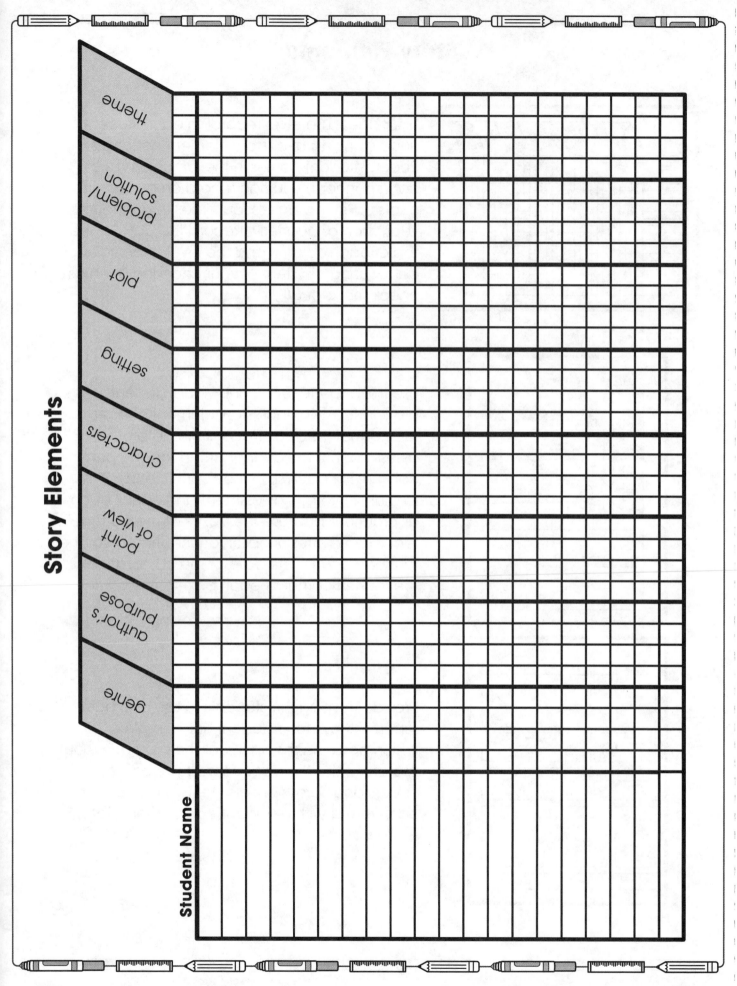

Student Name	genre	author's purpose	point of view	characters	setting	plot	problem/ solution	theme

Name: _____

Story Elements

				Identifies if a text is fiction or nonfiction
				Identifies genre
				Identifies author's purpose
				Identifies point of view
				Identifies characters
				Gives details about the characters
				Identifies setting
				Gives details about the setting
				Identifies the problem and solution
				Gives key events in order and can identify the most important event
				Identifies theme

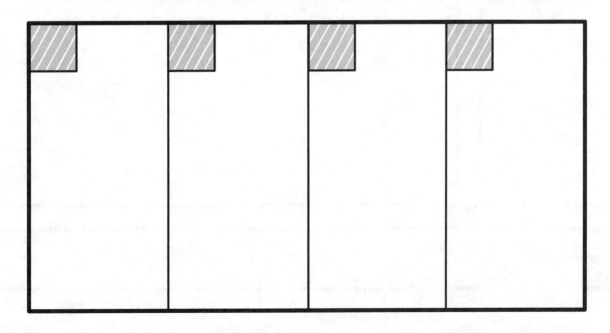

Story Elements

Title _____

Author _____   Illustrator _____

☐ fiction

☐ nonfiction

Genre _____

☐ first person
☐ second person
☐ third person

Identifying Pronouns _____

_____

Main Characters

Author's Purpose

P   I   E

Setting

Problem _____

_____

_____

_____

Solution _____

_____

_____

_____

Plot
List the key events in order. Circle the most important event.

Theme _____

Prose, Poetry, and Drama

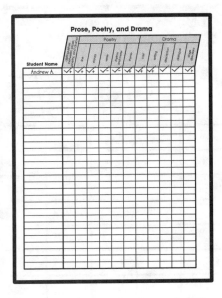

This page is useful for recording your class's proficiency with prose, poetry, and drama terms and skills. Record student names in the first column. Using either formal or informal assessments and a scale of your choosing, record individual student proficiencies for each skill or term. Note: *Rhyme* can refer to identifying rhymes or rhyme schemes.

This page allows for individual assessment of students' ability to differentiate between the three main forms of literature. Have students choose a piece of literature and record the title. Then, have students circle the type of literature and complete the reasoning section. Students should date and rate their work in the box at the bottom of each section. Use the *Notes* section to record any observations. If desired, divide the page in half and use as a pretest and posttest or as a test and retest.

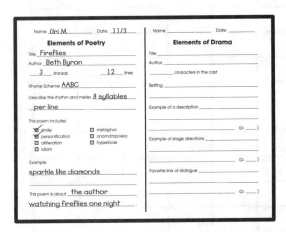

Use this page to assess students' understanding of the elements of poetry and drama. Cut the page in half and provide the relevant half depending on which type of literature is being studied or provide one sheet to each student and have students fill out the relevant side on different dates. Have students complete the prompts about a recently read piece of literature to prove their understanding.

Prose, Poetry and Drama

Student Name	distinguishes between prose, poetry, and drama	Poetry					Drama				
		line	stanza	verse	rhythm and meter	rhyme	cast	setting	description	dialogue	stage directions

Identifying Prose, Poetry, and Drama

Title _____

prose   **poetry**   **drama**

I know because _____

_____

_____

_____ .

Title _____

prose   **poetry**   **drama**

I know because _____

_____

_____

_____ .

Title _____

prose   **poetry**   **drama**

I know because _____

_____

_____

_____ .

Title _____

prose   **poetry**   **drama**

I know because _____

_____

_____

_____ .

Notes _____

_____

_____

 I don't understand yet.

 I can categorize literature with help.

 I can categorize literature correctly.

 I can teach it to others.

Elements of Drama

Title _____

Author _____

_____ characters in the cast

Setting _____

Example of a description

_____

_____ (p. ___)

Example of stage directions

_____ (p. ___)

Favorite line of dialogue

_____ (p. ___)

Elements of Poetry

Title _____

Author _____

_____ stanzas _____ lines

Rhyme Scheme _____

Describe the rhythm and meter.

_____

This poem includes

☐ simile   ☐ metaphor

☐ personification   ☐ onomatopoeia

☐ alliteration   ☐ hyperbole

☐ idiom

Example _____

This poem is about _____

Reading: Informational Text
Standards Crosswalk

Third Grade

Key Ideas and Details

- Refer to text to ask and answer questions to demonstrate understanding.
- Determine the main idea of a text.
- Recount key details and explain how they support the main idea.
- Use appropriate language (time, sequence, cause and effect) to describe the relationship between a series of historical events, scientific ideas or concepts, or steps in technical procedures in a text.

Craft and Structure

- Determine the meaning of general academic and domain-specific words and phrases.
- Use text features and search tools (key words, sidebars, hyperlinks) to locate information.
- Distinguish their own points of view from that of the author of a text.

Integration of Knowledge and Ideas

- Use information gained from illustrations and the words in a text to demonstrate understanding.
- Describe the logical connection between sentences and paragraphs in a text.
- Compare and contrast important points and key details from two texts on the same topic.

Range of Reading and Level of Text Complexity

- By the end of the year, read and comprehend informational texts independently at the high end of the grades 2–3 text complexity band independently and proficiently.

Fifth Grade

Key Ideas and Details

- Quote direct evidence from a text to explain and draw inferences.
- Determine two or more main ideas and details of a text.
- Summarize the text.
- Explain how people, events, ideas, or concepts are connected in a historical, scientific, or technical text.

Craft and Structure

- Determine the meaning of general academic and domain-specific words and phrases in a text relevant to a grade 5 topic or subject area.
- Compare and contrast the organizational structures in two or more texts.
- Describe how point of view affects descriptions of events.

Integration of Knowledge and Ideas

- Analyze how visual and multimedia elements contribute to the meaning, tone, or beauty of a text.
- Compare and contrast the approach to similar themes and topics in stories from the same genre.

Range of Reading and Level of Text Complexity

- By the end of the year, independently read and comprehend literature at the high end of the grades 4–5 text complexity band.

Reading: Informational Text
Concepts Checklist

Concept		Date(s) Taught				

Reading Informational Text

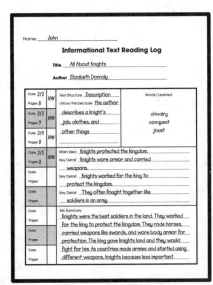

Use this page as a take-home reading log for informational texts. Each student should use one page for a single book, article, or other nonfiction text he reads at home. Each night, have him record the date and number of pages read along the left side. A family member should initial to the right. Then, as the student progresses through the book, she should complete the right-hand side of the page with information about the book.

Use this page for informal student reading conferences. As you conference with a student, record the student's name, the date, the book title, and the student's current reading level. Record the focus of the conference and any observed strengths and weaknesses. If desired, copy this page on adhesive label sheets to keep on a clipboard (visit our website for a free downloadable template). This makes conferencing and moving logs to student folders quick and easy. This page can also be used for literature conferencing.

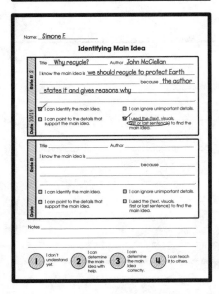

This page is useful for spotchecking students' understanding of main idea throughout the year. Have the student date the left side and complete the prompts about a book or text they have recently read. Then, have them check off the skills they feel confident about and rate their work using the 1–4 scale provided at the bottom of the page. This page can also be used for literature texts.

Name: _____

Informational Text Reading Log

Title _____

Author _____

Date		Text Structure _____	Words I Learned
Pages		I know this because _____	
Date			
Pages		_____	
Date		_____	
Pages		_____ .	

Date		Main Idea _____
Pages		Key Detail _____
		_____
Date		Key Detail _____
Pages		_____
Date		Key Detail _____
Pages		_____

Date		My Summary
Pages		_____
Date		_____
Pages		_____
Date		_____
Pages		_____

Informal Reading Conference Notes

Name _____ Date _____

Title _____ Level _____

Focus

Strengths | Goals

Name _____ Date _____

Title _____ Level _____

Focus

Strengths | Goals

Name _____ Date _____

Title _____ Level _____

Focus

Strengths | Goals

Name _____ Date _____

Title _____ Level _____

Focus

Strengths | Goals

Name: _____

Identifying Main Idea

Title _____ Author _____

I know the main idea is _____

_____ because _____

_____

_____.

☐ I can identify the main idea.   ☐ I can ignore unimportant details.

☐ I can point to the details that   ☐ I used the (text, visuals,
support the main idea.   first or last sentence) to find the
                                            main idea.

Rate It

Date

Title _____ Author _____

I know the main idea is _____

_____ because _____

_____

_____.

☐ I can identify the main idea.   ☐ I can ignore unimportant details.

☐ I can point to the details that   ☐ I used the (text, visuals,
support the main idea.   first or last sentence) to find the
                                            main idea.

Rate It

Date

Notes _____

_____

_____

1 I don't understand yet.   **2** I can determine the main idea with help.   **3** I can determine the main idea correctly.   **4** I can teach it to others.

Text Structure

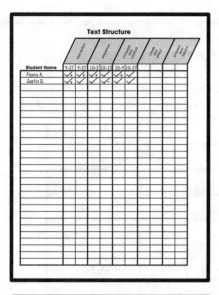

This page is useful for recording students' understanding of the different text structures. Record student names in the left column. For each text structure, you can record an assessment of a student's progress twice, such as with a pretest and posttest or a test and retest. Record the date at the top of each column and the level of proficiency below using a system of your choosing, such as check marks or E/P/M.

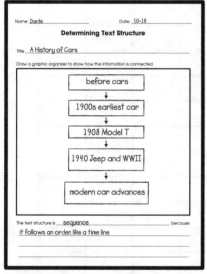

Provide this page to students to assess individual understanding of text structure. Have the student record the title of the text he is using and draw a graphic organizer to demonstrate how the information is connected and determine the text's overall structure. Then, have the student complete the prompt at the bottom of the page to show their reasoning.

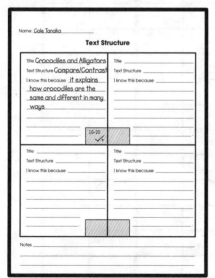

This page allows for individual assessment of text structure. Have students record the title of a text they have read recently and its text structure. Then, have students complete the reasoning prompt. Have students date their work in the box at the bottom of each section. If desired, use the same space to add a proficiency rating of your choosing. Use the *Notes* section to record any observations. If desired, divide the page in half and use as a pretest and posttest or as a test and retest, or use it four times throughout the year as a quarterly assessment.

Text Structure

Student Name	description		sequence		compare and contrast		cause and effect		problem and solution	

Determining Text Structure

Title _____

Draw a graphic organizer to show how the information is connected.

The text structure is _____ because

_____

_____

_____ .

Name: _____

Text Structure

Title _____

Text Structure _____

I know this because _____

_____

_____

_____

_____

_____ .

Title _____

Text Structure _____

I know this because _____

_____

_____

_____

_____

_____ .

Title _____

Text Structure _____

I know this because _____

_____

_____

_____

_____

_____ .

Title _____

Text Structure _____

I know this because _____

_____

_____

_____

_____

_____ .

Notes _____

_____

_____

Nonfiction Text Features

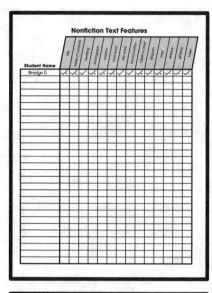

This page is useful for recording your class's proficiency with nonfiction text features. Using either formal or informal assessments and a scale of your choosing, record each student's mastery of each term.

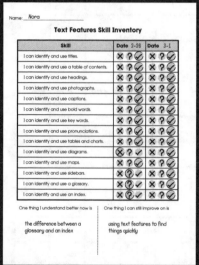

Use this page to help students keep track of their learning during a unit on nonfiction text features. Before the unit, have students complete the first column by adding the date, and then circling, coloring, or highlighting the appropriate symbol for each I Can . . . statement. An *X* means *not yet*, a *?* means *maybe*, and a ✔ means *yes*. Then, after the unit, have students repeat with the second column and answer the prompts at the bottom of the page to assess their overall learning.

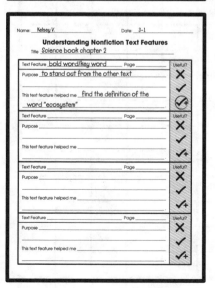

This page allows for individual assessment of identifying and using text features. Have students record the title of a text they have recently read. Then, students should complete a text feature scavenger hunt by finding four different text features in the text and using them to complete the prompts. Have students rate how useful they found each text feature by circling the appropriate symbol on the right-hand side of each row.

Nonfiction Text Features

Student Name	title	table of contents	heading	photograph	caption	bold word	key word	pronunciation	table or chart	diagram	map	sidebar	glossary	index

Name: _____

Text Features Skill Inventory

Skill	Date	Date
I can identify and use titles.	✗ ? ✓	✗ ? ✓
I can identify and use a table of contents.	✗ ? ✓	✗ ? ✓
I can identify and use headings.	✗ ? ✓	✗ ? ✓
I can identify and use photographs.	✗ ? ✓	✗ ? ✓
I can identify and use captions.	✗ ? ✓	✗ ? ✓
I can identify and use bold words.	✗ ? ✓	✗ ? ✓
I can identify and use key words.	✗ ? ✓	✗ ? ✓
I can identify and use pronunciations.	✗ ? ✓	✗ ? ✓
I can identify and use tables and charts.	✗ ? ✓	✗ ? ✓
I can identify and use diagrams.	✗ ? ✓	✗ ? ✓
I can identify and use maps.	✗ ? ✓	✗ ? ✓
I can identify and use sidebars.	✗ ? ✓	✗ ? ✓
I can identify and use a glossary.	✗ ? ✓	✗ ? ✓
I can identify and use an index.	✗ ? ✓	✗ ? ✓

One thing I understand better now is

One thing I can still improve on is

Name: _____   Date: _____

Understanding Nonfiction Text Features

Title _____

	Useful?
Text Feature _____ Page _____	✗
Purpose _____	✓
_____	
This text feature helped me _____	✓+
_____	

	Useful?
Text Feature _____ Page _____	✗
Purpose _____	✓
_____	
This text feature helped me _____	✓+
_____	

	Useful?
Text Feature _____ Page _____	✗
Purpose _____	✓
_____	
This text feature helped me _____	✓+
_____	

	Useful?
Text Feature _____ Page _____	✗
Purpose _____	✓
_____	
This text feature helped me _____	✓+
_____	

Reading: Foundational Skills
Standards Crosswalk

Third Grade

Phonics and Word Recognition

• Decode words using grade-level phonics and word analysis skills.
• Identify and know the meaning of most common prefixes and suffixes.
• Decode words with common Latin suffixes.
• Decode multisyllabic words.
• Read grade-appropriate, irregularly spelled words.

Fluency

• Read with sufficient accuracy and fluency to support comprehension.
• Read grade-level text with purpose and understanding.
• Read grade-level prose and poetry with accuracy, appropriate rate, and expression on successive readings.
• Use context and rereading to confirm or self-correct word recognition and understanding.

Fifth Grade

Phonics and Word Recognition

• Know and apply grade-level phonics and word analysis skills to decode words.
• Use all letter-sound correspondences, syllabication patterns, and morphology to read accurately unfamiliar multisyllabic words in context and out of context.

Fluency

• Read with sufficient accuracy and fluency to support comprehension.
• Read grade-level text with purpose and understanding.
• Read grade-level prose and poetry orally with accuracy, appropriate rate, and expression on successive readings.
• Use context and rereading to confirm or self-correct word recognition and understanding.

Reading: Foundational Skills
Concepts Checklist

Concept		Date(s) Taught			

Fluency

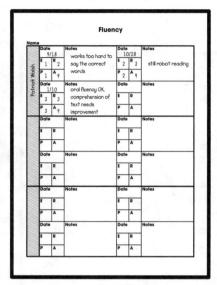

This page is useful for recording a student's level of fluency throughout the year. Record student names in the left column. You can record an assessment of a student's progress four times, once for each quarter (or more often if needed). Record the date at the top of each section. Also record the level of proficiency for each component of fluency (expression, rate, phrasing, and accuracy) using a system of your choosing, such as a rubric scale, check marks, or E/P/M. Use the *Notes* sections to record any observations.

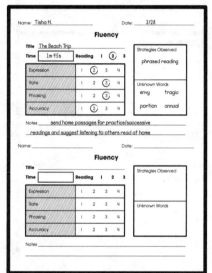

Use this page to asses each student's fluency more in-depth. As students read a passage of your choosing, record the title, the time it takes the student to complete the passage (or the time limit given), and whether it is the first, second, or third reading of that passage. Use the 1–4 scale to quickly assess each component of the student's performance. Record any strategies you observed the student use and any words they struggled with in the space to the right. Use the *Notes* section to record any additional observations.

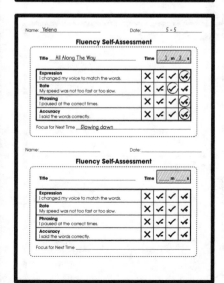

This page allows students to self-assess their fluency. After students read to you for fluency, provide them with this page. Or, provide a copy to send home to allow parents to help assess progress with fluency. Students should record the title and the time it took them to read the passage. Then, have students rate each component of their performance by circling the appropriate symbol to the right. Allow students to choose a focus for the next passage, or decide on a future focus together during a conference. This page can also be used to allow partners to assess each other's fluency with a passage.

Name: _____

Fluency

Name

	Date	Notes	Date	Notes
	E · R		E · R	
	P · A		P · A	
	Date	Notes	Date	Notes
	E · R		E · R	
	P · A		P · A	
	Date	Notes	Date	Notes
	E · R		E · R	
	P · A		P · A	
	Date	Notes	Date	Notes
	E · R		E · R	
	P · A		P · A	
	Date	Notes	Date	Notes
	E · R		E · R	
	P · A		P · A	
	Date	Notes	Date	Notes
	E · R		E · R	
	P · A		P · A	

Name: _____   Date: _____

Fluency

Title _____

Time [   ]   **Reading**   1   2   3

Expression	1	2	3	4
Rate	1	2	3	4
Phrasing	1	2	3	4
Accuracy	1	2	3	4

Strategies Observed

Unknown Words

Notes _____

_____

Name: _____   Date: _____

Fluency

Title _____

Time [   ]   **Reading**   1   2   3

Expression	1	2	3	4
Rate	1	2	3	4
Phrasing	1	2	3	4
Accuracy	1	2	3	4

Strategies Observed

Unknown Words

Notes _____

_____

Name: _____   Date: _____

Fluency Self-Assessment

Title _____   Time ⬜ ____ m ____ s

Expression I changed my voice to match the words.	✗	✓-	✓	✓+
Rate My speed was not too fast or too slow.	✗	✓-	✓	✓+
Phrasing I paused at the correct times.	✗	✓-	✓	✓+
Accuracy I said the words correctly.	✗	✓-	✓	✓+

Focus for Next Time _____

Name: _____   Date: _____

Fluency Self-Assessment

Title _____   Time ⬜ ____ m ____ s

Expression I changed my voice to match the words.	✗	✓-	✓	✓+
Rate My speed was not too fast or too slow.	✗	✓-	✓	✓+
Phrasing I paused at the correct times.	✗	✓-	✓	✓+
Accuracy I said the words correctly.	✗	✓-	✓	✓+

Focus for Next Time _____

Decoding Words

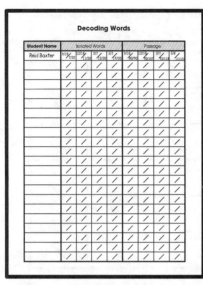

Use this page to track individual student progress and proficiency with decoding words. As you assess students on their ability to decode isolated words or as students read a passage, record the date and note the amount of correct words out of the total number of words assessed. Four spaces are provided for quarterly assessment during the year.

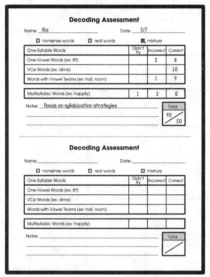

Use this page to conduct a more in-depth assessment of each student's word decoding skills. Before the assessment, choose prompt words (nonsense, real, or a mixture of both) and write or type them on a page or on index cards. Record the type of words used for the assessment. As you present the student with the words, record how she performed with each set in the appropriate space on the chart. It may help to sort the words into piles as they are read. Record the number of words correct out of the total number of words given. Use the *Notes* section to record any observations.

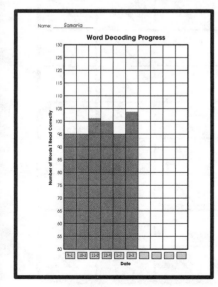

Allow students to track their own progress with reading passages on this page. As students read passages for fluency, have them record the date and add a bar showing how many words they said correctly in one minute.

Decoding Words

Student Name	Isolated Words				Passage			
	/	/	/	/	/	/	/	/
	/	/	/	/	/	/	/	/
	/	/	/	/	/	/	/	/
	/	/	/	/	/	/	/	/
	/	/	/	/	/	/	/	/
	/	/	/	/	/	/	/	/
	/	/	/	/	/	/	/	/
	/	/	/	/	/	/	/	/
	/	/	/	/	/	/	/	/
	/	/	/	/	/	/	/	/
	/	/	/	/	/	/	/	/
	/	/	/	/	/	/	/	/
	/	/	/	/	/	/	/	/
	/	/	/	/	/	/	/	/
	/	/	/	/	/	/	/	/
	/	/	/	/	/	/	/	/
	/	/	/	/	/	/	/	/
	/	/	/	/	/	/	/	/
	/	/	/	/	/	/	/	/
	/	/	/	/	/	/	/	/
	/	/	/	/	/	/	/	/

Name: _____   Date: _____

Decoding Assessment

☐ nonsense words   ☐ real words   ☐ mixture

One-Syllable Words	Didn't Try	Incorrect	Correct
One-Vowel Words (ex: lift)			
VCe Words (ex: dime)			
Words with Vowel Teams (ex: hail, room)			

Multisyllabic Words (ex: happily)			

Notes _____

_____

_____

Total
╱

Name: _____   Date: _____

Decoding Assessment

☐ nonsense words   ☐ real words   ☐ mixture

One-Syllable Words	Didn't Try	Incorrect	Correct
One-Vowel Words (ex: lift)			
VCe Words (ex: dime)			
Words with Vowel Teams (ex: hail, room)			

Multisyllabic Words (ex: happily)			

Notes _____

_____

_____

Total
╱

Name: _____

Word Decoding Progress

Number of Words I Read Correctly

130
125
120
115
110
105
100
95
90
85
80
75
70
65
60
55
50

Date

Writing
Standards Crosswalk

Third Grade

Text Types and Purposes
- Write opinion pieces, supporting a point of view with reasons.
- Introduce the topic or text, state an opinion, and list reasons to support the opinion in an organized manner; use linking words and phrases to connect opinion and reasons; provide a concluding statement.
- Write informative/explanatory texts to examine a topic and convey ideas and information clearly.
- Introduce a topic, group related information, and include illustrations when useful; develop the topic with facts, definitions, and details; use linking words and phrases to connect ideas; provide a concluding statement or section.
- Write real or imaginary narratives using effective technique, details, and clear sequences.
- Establish a situation and introduce a narrator and/or characters; organize a sequence of events; use dialogue, and describe the actions, thoughts and feelings of characters in response to situations; use temporal words and phrases to signal event order; provide closure.

Production and Distribution of Writing
With guidance and support:
- Develop, organize, and produce writing appropriate to task and purpose.
- Develop and strengthen writing by planning, revising, and editing.
- Use technology to produce and publish writing (using keyboarding skills), including in collaboration.

Research to Build and Present Knowledge
- Conduct research to build knowledge about a topic.
- Recall information from experiences or gather information from print and digital sources.
- Take brief notes on sources and sort evidence into provided categories.

Range of Writing
- Routinely write for a range of discipline-specific tasks, purposes, and audiences.

Fifth Grade

Text Types and Purposes
- Write opinion pieces, supporting a point of view with reasons and information.
- Introduce the topic or text clearly, state an opinion, and use an organized structure that groups related ideas; provide logically-ordered reasons supported by facts and details; use linking words, phrases, and clauses to connect opinion and reasons; provide a related conclusion.
- Write informative/explanatory texts to examine a topic and convey ideas and information clearly.
- Introduce a topic clearly; provide a general observation and focus, group related information in paragraphs and sections and include formatting, illustrations, and multimedia when useful; develop the topic with facts, definitions, concrete details, quotations, and other relevant information; use linking words, phrases, and clauses to connect ideas; provide a related conclusion.
- Write real or imaginary narratives using effective technique, details, and clear sequences.
- Establish a situation and introduce a narrator and/or characters; organize a sequence of events; use dialogue, description, and pacing to develop experiences, events, and characters' responses to situations; use transitional words, phrases, and clauses to manage the sequence of events; use concrete words, phrases, and sensory details to convey experiences and events; provide a logical conclusion.

Production and Distribution of Writing
- Produce coherent writing with development and organization appropriate to task and purpose.
- With guidance and support, develop and strengthen writing by planning, revising, editing, or rewriting.
- With some guidance and support, use technology to produce and publish writing and to interact and collaborate; demonstrate sufficient keyboarding skills to type at least two pages in a sitting.

Research to Build and Present Knowledge
- Conduct short research projects using several sources that build knowledge about a topic.
- Recall relevant information from experiences or gather information from print and digital sources.
- Summarize or paraphrase information in notes and writing, and provide a list of sources.
- Draw evidence from texts to support analysis, reflection, and research.

Range of Writing
- Routinely write for a range of discipline-specific tasks, purposes, and audiences.

Writing Concepts Checklist

Concept		Date(s) Taught				

Opinion Writing

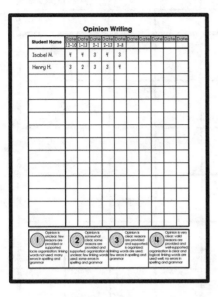

This page is useful for recording students' opinion writing scores. Record student names in the left column. Record the date at the top of each column. Then, record the level of proficiency using the 1–4 rubric at the bottom of the page as a guide, or with a different system of your choosing. Keep the graded samples of students' work in writing portfolios to refer back to.

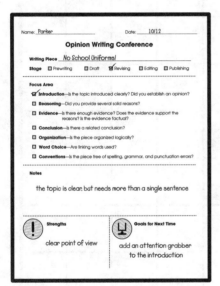

Use this page for student conferences. Choose the correct page for the student's writing piece (find conference forms for informative writing on page 115 and narrative writing on page 119). Use the form to guide the conference. Record the date, the topic or title of the writing piece, and the stage the piece is in. Then, choose a focus area for the conference. Use the *Notes* section to record any observations. Work with the student to record strengths observed in the piece and goals for next time.

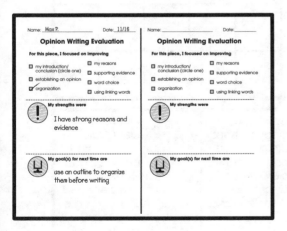

Provide this page to students to help them evaluate their opinion writing pieces (find self-assessment forms for informative writing on page 116 and narrative writing on page 120). Have students complete the prompts based on a finished opinion piece. Store the student's self-assessment with the writing piece.

Opinion Writing

Student Name	Date	Date	Date	Date	Date	Date	Date	Date	Date	Date

 Opinion is unclear; few reasons are provided or supported; lacks organization; linking words not used; many errors in spelling and grammar

 Opinion is somewhat clear; some reasons are provided and supported; organization is unclear; few linking words used; some errors in spelling and grammar

 Opinion is clear; reasons are provided and supported; is organized; linking words are used; few errors in spelling and grammar

 Opinion is very clear; valid reasons are provided and well-supported; organization is clear and logical; linking words are used well; no errors in spelling and grammar

Name: _____ Date: _____

Opinion Writing Conference

Writing Piece _____

Stage ☐ Prewriting ☐ Draft ☐ Revising ☐ Editing ☐ Publishing

- -

Focus Area

☐ **Introduction**—Is the topic introduced clearly? Did you establish an opinion?

☐ **Reasoning**—Did you provide several solid reasons?

☐ **Evidence**—Is there enough evidence? Does the evidence support the reasons? Is the evidence factual?

☐ **Conclusion**—Is there a related conclusion?

☐ **Organization**—Is the piece organized logically?

☐ **Word Choice**—Are linking words used?

☐ **Conventions**—Is the piece free of spelling, grammar, and punctuation errors?

- -

Notes

- -

Strengths

Goals for Next Time

Name: _____ Date: _____

Opinion Writing Evaluation

For this piece, I focused on improving

- ☐ my introduction/ conclusion (circle one)
- ☐ establishing an opinion
- ☐ organization
- ☐ my reasons
- ☐ supporting evidence
- ☐ word choice
- ☐ using linking words

My strengths were

My goal(s) for next time are

Name: _____ Date: _____

Opinion Writing Evaluation

For this piece, I focused on improving

- ☐ my introduction/ conclusion (circle one)
- ☐ establishing an opinion
- ☐ organization
- ☐ my reasons
- ☐ supporting evidence
- ☐ word choice
- ☐ using linking words

My strengths were

My goal(s) for next time are

Informative Writing

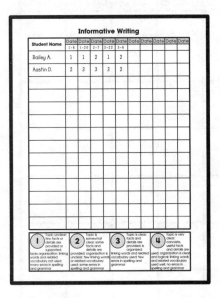

This page is useful for recording students' informative writing scores. Record student names in the left column. Record the date at the top of each column. Then, record the level of proficiency using the 1–4 rubric at the bottom of the page as a guide, or with a different system of your choosing. Keep the graded samples of students' work in writing portfolios to refer back to.

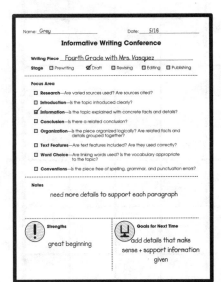

Use this page for student conferences. Choose the correct page for the student's writing piece (find conference forms for opinion writing on page 111 and narrative writing on page 119). Use the form to guide the conference. Record the date, the topic or title of the writing piece, and the stage the piece is in. Then, choose a focus area for the conference. Use the *Notes* section to record any observations. Work with the student to record strengths observed in the piece and goals for next time.

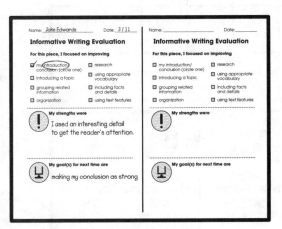

Provide this page to students to help them evaluate their informative writing pieces (find self-assessment forms for opinion writing on page 112 and narrative writing on page 120). Have students complete the prompts based on a finished informative piece. Store the student's self-assessment with the completed writing piece.

Informative Writing

Student Name	Date	Date	Date	Date	Date	Date	Date	Date	Date	Date

 Topic unclear; few facts or details are provided or supported; lacks organization; linking words and related vocabulary not used; many errors in spelling and grammar

 Topic is somewhat clear; some facts and details are provided; organization is unclear; few linking words or related vocabulary used; some errors in spelling and grammar

 Topic is clear; facts and details are provided; is organized; linking words and related vocabulary used; few errors in spelling and grammar

 Topic is very clear; concrete, useful facts and details are used; organization is clear and logical; linking words and related vocabulary used well; no errors in spelling and grammar

Name: _____   Date: _____

Informative Writing Conference

Writing Piece _____

Stage   ☐ Prewriting   ☐ Draft   ☐ Revising   ☐ Editing   ☐ Publishing

---

Focus Area

☐ **Research**—Are varied sources used? Are sources cited?

☐ **Introduction**—Is the topic introduced clearly?

☐ **Information**—Is the topic explained with concrete facts and details?

☐ **Conclusion**—Is there a related conclusion?

☐ **Organization**—Is the piece organized logically? Are related facts and details grouped together?

☐ **Text Features**—Are text features included? Are they used correctly?

☐ **Word Choice**—Are linking words used? Is the vocabulary appropriate to the topic?

☐ **Conventions**—Is the piece free of spelling, grammar, and punctuation errors?

Notes

Strengths

Goals for Next Time

Informative Writing Evaluation

Name: _____ Date: _____

For this piece, I focused on improving

- ☐ my introduction/conclusion (circle one)
- ☐ research
- ☐ introducing a topic
- ☐ using appropriate vocabulary
- ☐ grouping related information
- ☐ including facts and details
- ☐ organization
- ☐ using text features

My strengths were

My goal(s) for next time are

Informative Writing Evaluation

Name: _____ Date: _____

For this piece, I focused on improving

- ☐ my introduction/conclusion (circle one)
- ☐ research
- ☐ introducing a topic
- ☐ using appropriate vocabulary
- ☐ grouping related information
- ☐ including facts and details
- ☐ organization
- ☐ using text features

My strengths were

My goal(s) for next time are

Narrative Writing

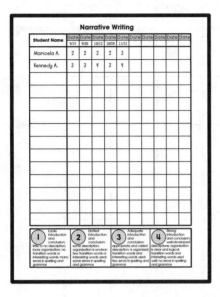

This page is useful for recording students' narrative writing scores. Record student names in the left column. Record the date at the top of each column. Then, record the level of proficiency using the 1–4 rubric at the bottom of the page as a guide, or with a different system of your choosing. Keep the graded samples of students' work in writing portfolios to refer back to.

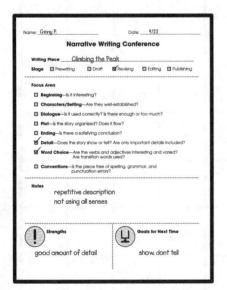

Use this page for student conferences. Choose the correct page for the student's writing piece (find conference forms for opinion writing on page 111 and informative writing on page 115). Use the form to guide the conference. Record the date, the topic or title of the writing piece, and the stage the piece is in. Then, choose a focus area for the conference. Use the *Notes* section to record any observations. Work with the student to record strengths observed in the piece and goals for next time.

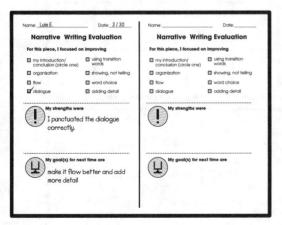

Provide this page to students to help them evaluate their own narrative writing pieces (find self-assessment forms for opinion writing on page 112 and informative writing on page 116). Have students complete the prompts based on a finished narrative piece. Store the student's self-assessment with the completed writing piece.

Narrative Writing

Student Name	Date	Date	Date	Date	Date	Date	Date	Date	Date	Date

1 Lacks introduction and conclusion; little to no description; lacks organization; no transition words or interesting words; many errors in spelling and grammar

2 Limited introduction and conclusion; some description; organization is unclear; few transition words or interesting words used; some errors in spelling and grammar

3 Adequate introduction and conclusion; appropriate and varied description; is organized; transition words and interesting words used; few errors in spelling and grammar

4 Strong introduction and conclusion; well-developed descriptions; organization is clear and logical; transition words and interesting words used well; no errors in spelling and grammar

Name: _____   Date: _____

Narrative Writing Conference

Writing Piece _____

Stage ☐ Prewriting   ☐ Draft   ☐ Revising   ☐ Editing   ☐ Publishing

----

Focus Area

☐ **Beginning**—Is it interesting?

☐ **Characters/Setting**—Are they well-established?

☐ **Dialogue**—Is it used correctly? Is there enough or too much?

☐ **Plot**—Is the story organized? Does it flow?

☐ **Ending**—Is there a satisfying conclusion?

☐ **Detail**—Does the story show or tell? Are only important details included?

☐ **Word Choice**—Are the verbs and adjectives interesting and varied?
     Are transition words used?

☐ **Conventions**—Is the piece free of spelling, grammar, and
     punctuation errors?

Notes

Strengths

Goals for Next Time

Name: _____   Date: _____

Narrative Writing Evaluation

For this piece, I focused on improving

- [ ] my introduction/ conclusion (circle one)
- [ ] organization
- [ ] flow
- [ ] dialogue

- [ ] using transition words
- [ ] showing, not telling
- [ ] word choice
- [ ] adding detail

My strengths were

My goal(s) for next time are

Name: _____   Date: _____

Narrative Writing Evaluation

For this piece, I focused on improving

- [ ] my introduction/ conclusion (circle one)
- [ ] organization
- [ ] flow
- [ ] dialogue

- [ ] using transition words
- [ ] showing, not telling
- [ ] word choice
- [ ] adding detail

My strengths were

My goal(s) for next time are

Evaluating Writing

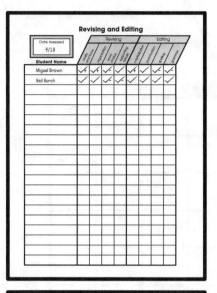

This page is useful for recording your class's proficiency with revising and editing tasks. Using either formal or informal assessments and a scale of your choosing, record individual student proficiencies for each task.

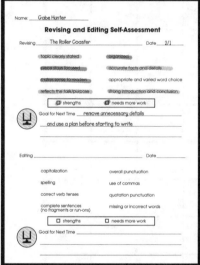

Provide this page to students to help them assess their ability to revise and edit their own writing. After each student revises or edits a piece of her writing, have her record the title of the piece and choose two colors to complete the key at the bottom of the appropriate section. She should then highlight or circle tasks she performed well and tasks she needs to work on more using the appropriate colors. Then, the student should record a goal to work on for next time. Store the student's self-assessment with the related writing piece.

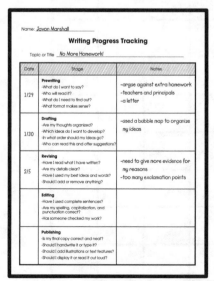

Allow students to use this progress tracking page to guide a piece of writing through the entire writing process. Have students record the title or topic of the piece at the top. As they reach each stage, they should add the date, use the questions in the *Stage* section to guide their thinking, and use the *Notes* section to add any relevant notes. If desired, use this page as part of your writing conferences to help students become comfortable with the process.

Revising and Editing

Student Name	Date Assessed	Revising				Editing			
		clarity and focus	organization	word choice	supporting details	capitalization	punctuation	spelling	grammar

Name: _____

Revising and Editing Self-Assessment

Revising _____ Date _____

topic clearly stated   organized

piece stays focused   accurate facts and details

makes sense to readers   appropriate and varied word choice

reflects the task/purpose   strong introduction and conclusion

☐ strengths	☐ needs more work

Goal for Next Time _____

_____

_____

Editing _____ Date _____

capitalization   overall punctuation

spelling   use of commas

correct verb tenses   quotation punctuation

complete sentences   missing or incorrect words
(no fragments or run-ons)

☐ strengths	☐ needs more work

Goal for Next Time _____

_____

_____

Name: _____

Writing Progress Tracking

Topic or Title _____

Date	Stage	Notes
	Prewriting -What do I want to say? -Who will read it? -What do I need to find out? -What format makes sense?	
	Drafting -Are my thoughts organized? -Which ideas do I want to develop? -In what order should my ideas go? -Who can read this and offer suggestions?	
	Revising -Have I read what I have written? -Are my details clear? -Have I used my best ideas and words? -Should I add or remove anything?	
	Editing -Have I used complete sentences? -Are my spelling, capitalization, and punctuation correct? -Has someone checked my work?	
	Publishing -Is my final copy correct and neat? -Should I handwrite it or type it? -Should I add illustrations or text features? -Should I display it or read it out loud?	

Speaking and Listening
Standards Crosswalk

Third Grade

Comprehension and Collaboration

• Participate in collaborative discussions on grade 3 topics and texts.
• Prepare for discussions and participate appropriately.
• Follow agreed-upon rules for discussions.
• Ask questions to clarify information presented, stay on topic, and offer relevant comments.
• Explain their own ideas and understanding in light of a discussion.
• Determine the main ideas and supporting details of a text read aloud or of multimedia presentations.
• Ask and answer questions about information from a speaker, offering appropriate elaboration.

Presentation of Knowledge and Ideas

• Speak clearly at an understandable pace to report on a topic or text, tell a story, or recount an experience with appropriate facts and descriptive details.
• Create audio recordings of stories or poems that demonstrate fluency and appropriate pacing.
• Add visual displays when needed to enhance certain facts or details.
• Speak in complete sentences when appropriate to provide requested detail or clarification.

Fifth Grade

Comprehension and Collaboration

• Participate in collaborative discussions on grade 5 topics and texts, building on others' ideas and expressing their own clearly.
• Come prepared to discussions, having read or studied material, drawing on that preparation to explore ideas under discussion.
• Follow agreed-upon rules for discussions and carry out assigned roles.
• Ask and answer questions and make comments that contribute to the discussion.
• Review the key ideas expressed and draw conclusions in light of the discussion.
• Summarize a written text read aloud or information presented in diverse media and formats.
• Summarize and explain the reasons and evidence supporting points a speaker makes.

Presentation of Knowledge and Ideas

• Report on a topic or text or present an opinion, sequencing ideas logically and using appropriate facts and relevant, descriptive details.
• Speak clearly at an understandable pace.
• Include multimedia components and visual displays in presentations when appropriate.
• Adapt speech to a variety of contexts and tasks, using formal English when appropriate.

Speaking and Listening Concepts Checklist

Concept		Date(s) Taught			

Discussion and Interaction

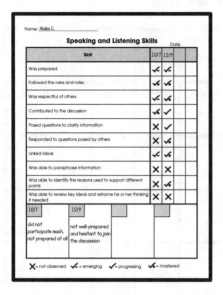

This page is useful for recording a student's performance during a class discussion or other types of interaction, such as book clubs. It can be used several times throughout the year to assess a student's progress. Record the date of the discussion at the top of the column. For each skill, draw the appropriate symbol to assess proficiency using the check mark system at the bottom of the page, or with another system of your choosing. Use the boxes at the bottom of the page to record any observations. Write the date in the top corner of each box.

Provide this page to students for goal-setting with speaking and listening skills. During individual conferences, work with the student to choose an appropriate goal and complete the prompts. Record the start date at the bottom of the page. Meet regularly to assess progress and record progress by circling the appropriate symbol in pencil. Finally, record the date once the goal has been accomplished.

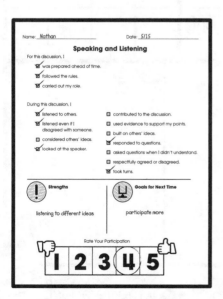

Students can use this page to self-assess their performance in discussions or in other group settings. Students should check off the item(s) they did during the discussion. Note that the second set of check boxes is divided into listening skills (left side) and speaking skills (right side) for ease of determining a student's areas of strength and weakness. Have students record their strengths and goals for next time at the bottom of the page and rate their overall performance by circling a number.

Name: _____

Speaking and Listening Skills

Date

Skill				
Was prepared				
Followed the rules and roles				
Was respectful of others				
Contributed to the discussion				
Posed questions to clarify information				
Responded to questions posed by others				
Linked ideas				
Was able to paraphrase information				
Was able to identify the reasons used to support different points				
Was able to review key ideas and reframe his or her thinking if needed				

X = not observed ✔- = emerging ✔ = progressing ✔+ = mastered

Speaking and Listening Goal

Name: _____

I would like to improve on _____

_____

To meet my goal, I will

- _____
- _____
- _____

START	GOAL!	
Start Date	Progress ✓⁻ ✓ ✓⁺	Achieved

Speaking and Listening Goal

Name: _____

I would like to improve on _____

_____

To meet my goal, I will

- _____
- _____
- _____

START	GOAL!	
Start Date	Progress ✓⁻ ✓ ✓⁺	Achieved

Name: _____ Date: _____

Speaking and Listening

For this discussion, I

☐ was prepared ahead of time.

☐ followed the rules.

☐ carried out my role.

During this discussion, I

☐ listened to others.

☐ listened even if I disagreed with someone.

☐ considered others' ideas.

☐ looked at the speaker.

☐ contributed to the discussion.

☐ used evidence to support my points.

☐ built on others' ideas.

☐ responded to questions.

☐ asked questions when I didn't understand.

☐ respectfully agreed or disagreed.

☐ took turns.

 Strengths

 Goals for Next Time

Rate Your Participation

 1 2 3 4 5

Presentation

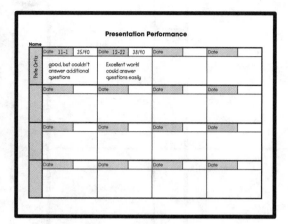

Use this page to track a student's progress with presentations throughout the year. Assess each student several times throughout the year, such as quarterly. Complete the top of each column by adding the date and then a rating of your choosing, such as a rubric score or check marks. Use the section below to record any notes and observations, such as the topic of the presentation, or strengths and goals.

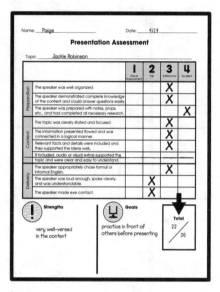

This page is useful for recording more detailed assessment information about a student's presentation. Mark an *X* in the appropriate column to rate the student's performance for each skill. If a skill was not demonstrated, such as using visuals, mark through it. Use the *Strengths* and *Goals* sections to record observations about the presentation, or complete it when conferencing with the student after the presentation. Record the score out of the total possible amount in the box at the bottom right of the page.

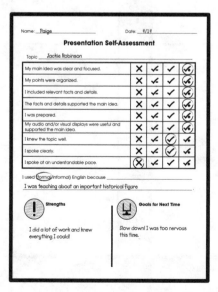

Provide students with a copy of this page after each presentation so they can assess their performance. Have students record the topic of their presentation and circle the appropriate symbol to rate themselves on each skill. Then, students should circle *formal* or *informal* to indicate the type of English they used, and justify their choice. Finally, have students record their strengths and their goals for the next presentation. You may choose to have students complete the bottom section during a conference about the presentation.

Presentation Performance

Name								
Date		Date		Date		Date		
Date		Date		Date		Date		
Date		Date		Date		Date		
Date		Date		Date		Date		

Name: _____ Date: _____

Presentation Assessment

Topic _____

		1 Needs Improvement	**2** Fair	**3** Satisfactory	**4** Excellent
Preparation	The speaker was well organized.				
	The speaker demonstrated complete knowledge of the content and could answer questions easily.				
	The speaker was prepared with notes, props, etc., and had completed all necessary research.				
Content	The topic was clearly stated and focused.				
	The information presented flowed and was connected in a logical manner.				
	Relevant facts and details were included and they supported the ideas well.				
	If included, audio or visual extras supported the topic and were clear and easy to understand.				
Delivery	The speaker appropriately chose formal or informal English.				
	The speaker was loud enough, spoke clearly, and was understandable.				
	The speaker made eye contact.				

 Strengths

 Goals

 **Total**

Name: _____ Date: _____

Presentation Self-Assessment

Topic _____

My main idea was clear and focused.	✗	✓−	✓	✓+
My points were organized.	✗	✓−	✓	✓+
I included relevant facts and details.	✗	✓−	✓	✓+
The facts and details supported the main idea.	✗	✓−	✓	✓+
I was prepared.	✗	✓−	✓	✓+
My audio and/or visual displays were useful and supported the main idea.	✗	✓−	✓	✓+
I knew the topic well.	✗	✓−	✓	✓+
I spoke clearly.	✗	✓−	✓	✓+
I spoke at an understandable pace.	✗	✓−	✓	✓+

I used (formal/informal) English because _____

_____

 Strengths

 Goals for Next Time

Language
Standards Crosswalk

Third Grade

Conventions of Standard English
- Use conventions of standard English grammar and usage in writing or speaking.
- Understand and explain the function of nouns, pronouns, verbs, adjectives, and adverbs; form and use regular and irregular plural nouns; use abstract nouns; form and use regular and irregular verbs, and simple verb tenses; ensure subject-verb and pronoun-antecedent agreement; form and use comparative and superlative adjectives and adverbs; use coordinating and subordinating conjunctions.
- Produce simple, compound, and complex sentences.
- Use capitalization, punctuation, and spelling correctly when writing.
- Capitalize appropriate words in titles; use commas in addresses; use commas and quotation marks in dialogue; form and use possessives.
- Use conventional spelling and spelling patterns to write words and to add suffixes to base words; consult reference materials to check and correct spellings.

Knowledge of Language
- Choose words and phrases for effect.
- Recognize differences between spoken and written standard English.

Vocabulary Acquisition and Use
- Flexibly use various strategies to understand unknown words on a third-grade level.
- Use sentence-level context as a clue to the meaning of a word or phrase; find the meaning of a new word when a known affix is added to a known word; use known root words to determine the meaning of an unknown word with same root; use glossaries or dictionaries to clarify meaning.
- Understand figurative language, word relationships, and nuances in words.
- Distinguish the literal and nonliteral meanings of words and phrases in context.
- Identify real-life connections between words and their uses.
- Distinguish meaning among words that describe states of mind or certainty.
- Correctly use conversational, academic, and subject-specific vocabulary, including words to show time and place.

Fifth Grade

Conventions of Standard English
- Use conventions of standard English grammar and usage in writing or speaking.
- Explain the function of conjunctions, prepositions, and interjections; form and use the perfect verb tenses; use verb tense to convey various times, sequences, states, and conditions; recognize and correct inappropriate shifts in verb tense; use correlative conjunctions.
- Use capitalization, punctuation, and spelling correctly when writing.
- Use punctuation to separate items in a series; use a comma to separate an introductory element from the rest of the sentence; use a comma to set off introductory words or phrases and questions, and to indicate direct address; use underlining, quotation marks, or italics to indicate titles of works.
- Spell grade-appropriate words correctly, consulting references as needed.

Knowledge of Language
- Use knowledge of language when writing, speaking, reading, or listening.
- Expand, combine, and reduce sentences for meaning, audience interest, and style.
- Compare and contrast the varieties of English used in stories, dramas, or poems.

Vocabulary Acquisition and Use
- Use various strategies to determine the meaning of unfamiliar words or phrases.
- Use context and common Greek and Latin affixes and roots as clues to the meaning of a word or phrase; consult reference materials to find the pronunciation and meaning of key words.
- Understand figurative language, word relationships, and nuances in word meaning in context; recognize the meanings of idioms, adages, and proverbs.
- Use the relationships between words to better understand each word.
- Learn and use academic and subject-specific vocabulary, including words that signal contrast, addition, and other logical relationships.

Language Concepts Checklist

Concept		Date(s) Taught				

Parts of Speech

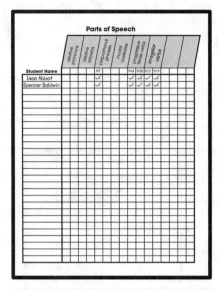

This page is useful for recording a student's overall understanding of the different parts of speech. Record student names in the left column. For each part of speech, you can record an assessment of a student's progress twice, such as with a pretest and posttest or a test and retest. Record the date at the top of each column and the level of proficiency below using a system of your choosing, such as check marks or E/P/M. Use the blank columns to add additional parts of speech as needed.

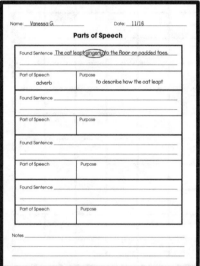

This page allows for individual assessment of understanding parts of speech. Challenge students to find four examples of the same part of speech or four different parts of speech. Students should look in a text to find the part of speech, record the sentence including it, underline or circle the word, identify the part of speech, and explain the purpose it serves in the sentence. Use the *Notes* section to record any observations. If desired, divide the page in half and use as a pretest and posttest or as a test and retest.

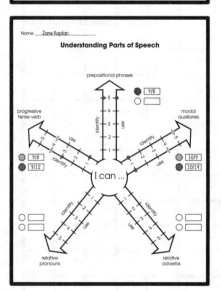

Use this page to allow students to record their understanding of different parts of speech. Before introducing a new part of speech, such as modal auxiliaries, have students color one circle beside the appropriate "arm" and record the date to create a key. Then, have the student use that color to add a dot showing their confidence with identifying and using that part of speech, on a scale from 1 (not at all confident) to 5 (very confident). After you teach a lesson on each part of speech, have students return to the page and repeat the process to see how their confidence levels have changed.

Parts of Speech

Student Name	relative pronouns	relative adverbs	prepositional phrases	modal auxiliaries	progressive tense verbs			

Parts of Speech

| Found Sentence _____ |
| _____ |

Part of Speech	Purpose

| Found Sentence _____ |
| _____ |

Part of Speech	Purpose

| Found Sentence _____ |
| _____ |

Part of Speech	Purpose

| Found Sentence _____ |
| _____ |

Part of Speech	Purpose

Notes _____

_____

_____

Understanding Parts of Speech

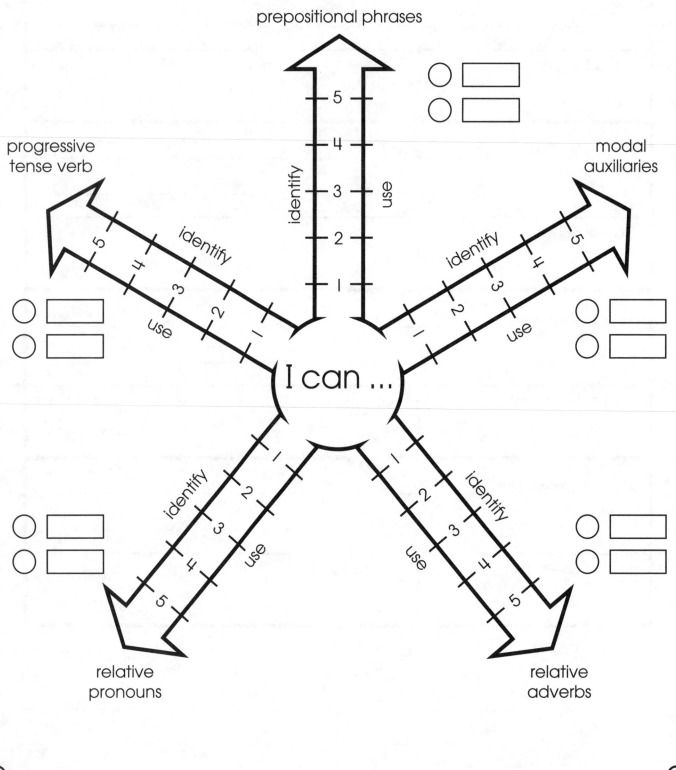

Spelling

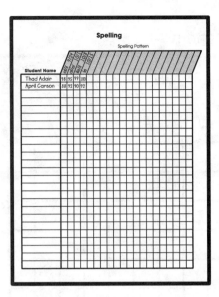

This page is useful for recording your class's proficiency with spelling patterns. Record student names in the left column and record the spelling patterns or other identifying information, such as test date, across the top. Using spelling tests and a scale of your choosing, record individual student proficiencies for each spelling pattern.

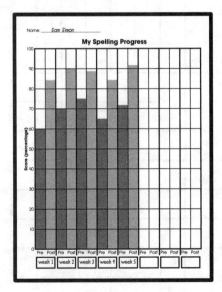

Provide this page to students for goal-setting with spelling patterns. During individual conferences, work with the student to choose an appropriate goal and complete the prompts. Record the date once the goal has been accomplished and have the student record words they can now spell to prove proficiency.

Allow students to track their own progress with spelling tests on this page. As students complete pretests and posttests, have them record the week, date, or spelling pattern and add a bar showing the percentage they got correct. If desired, have students use different colors to show pretest and posttest scores.

Spelling

Spelling Pattern

Student Name

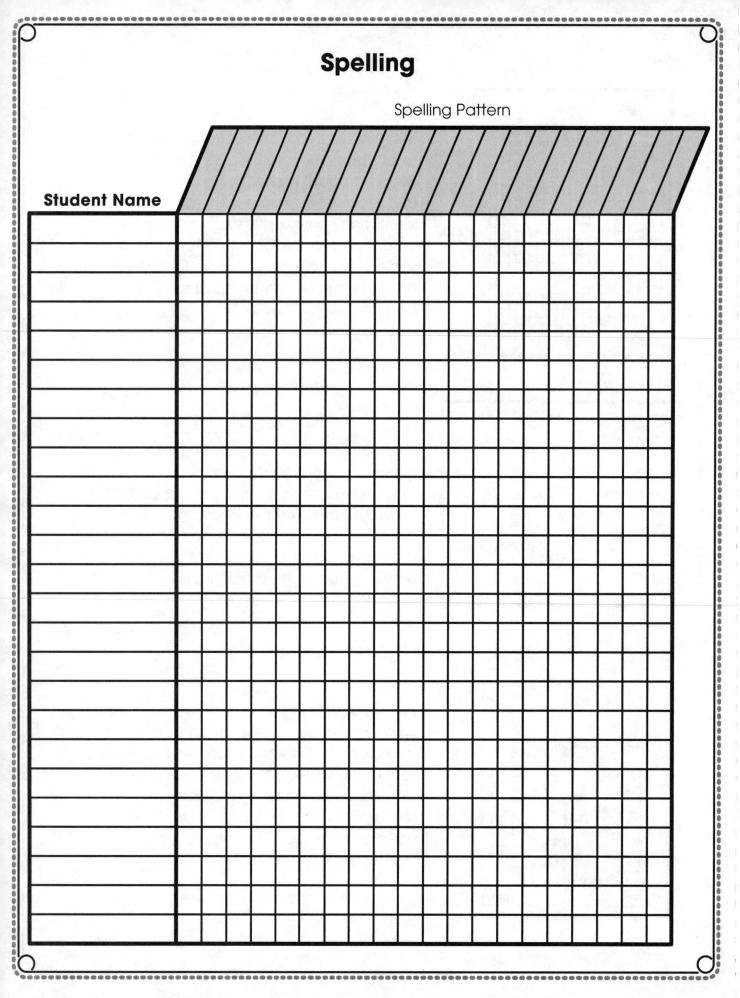

My Spelling Goal

Name: _____

Date: _____

I will _____

My Action Plan

- _____
- _____
- _____

⭐ I achieved my goal!

Words I Can Spell Now

My Spelling Goal

Name: _____

Date: _____

I will _____

My Action Plan

- _____
- _____
- _____

⭐ I achieved my goal!

Words I Can Spell Now

Name: _____

My Spelling Progress

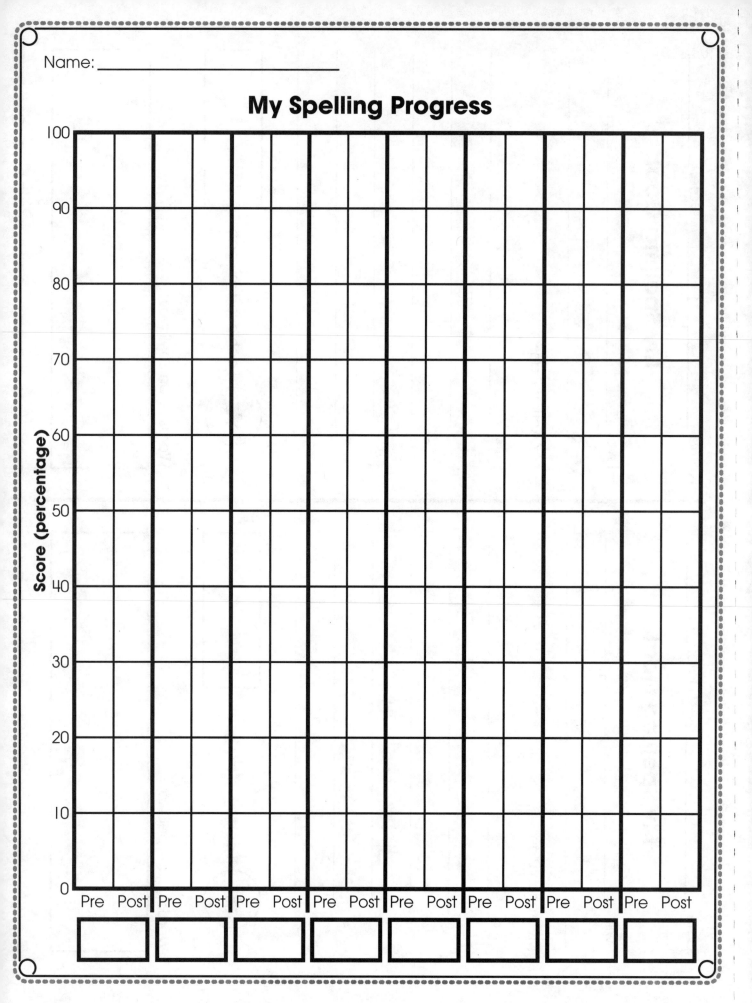

Score (percentage)

100
90
80
70
60
50
40
30
20
10
0

| Pre | Post | Pre | Post | Pre | Post | Pre | Post | Pre | Post | Pre | Post | Pre | Post | Pre | Post |

Punctuation and Capitalization

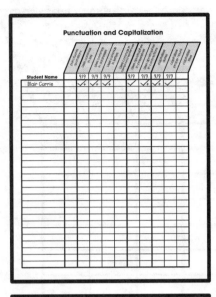

This page is useful for recording a student's understanding of punctuation and capitalization concepts. Record student names in the left column. For each concept, you can record the date it was taught or assessed at the top of the column or you may choose to leave it blank if using informal assessment at different points in the year. Record the level of proficiency below using a system of your choosing, such as check marks or E/P/M.

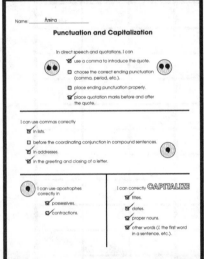

Provide students with this page to help them track and celebrate their understanding of correct capitalization and punctuation. As students master each skill, they should check off the appropriate box. If desired, have students add a date beside the description to record when they mastered the skill.

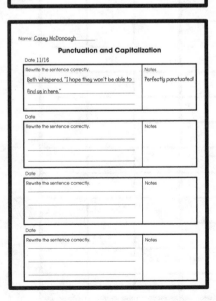

Use this page to assess individual students' success with punctuation and capitalization rules. Provide students with an incorrect sentence, and have them record the corrected version on the page. Use the *Notes* section to record any observations. If desired, use this page all at one time to provide a snapshot, or once per quarter to create a portfolio of progress for the year.

Punctuation and Capitalization

Student Name	punctuates quotations	Uses commas in lists	Uses commas in addresses	Uses commas in letters	Uses commas in compound sentences	Uses apostrophes in possessives	Uses apostrophes in contractions	capitalizes dates	capitalizes proper nouns	capitalizes titles

Name: _____

Punctuation and Capitalization

In direct speech and quotations, I can

- ☐ use a comma to introduce the quote.

- ☐ choose the correct ending punctuation (comma, period, etc.).

- ☐ place ending punctuation properly.

- ☐ place quotation marks before and after the quote.

I can use commas correctly

- ☐ in lists.

- ☐ before the coordinating conjunction in compound sentences.

- ☐ in addresses.

- ☐ in the greeting and closing of a letter.

 I can use apostrophes correctly in

- ☐ possessives.

- ☐ contractions.

I can correctly CAPITALIZE

- ☐ titles.

- ☐ dates.

- ☐ proper nouns.

- ☐ other words (*I*, the first word in a sentence, etc.).

Punctuation and Capitalization

Date

Rewrite the sentence correctly.	Notes
_____ _____ _____	

Date

Rewrite the sentence correctly.	Notes
_____ _____ _____	

Date

Rewrite the sentence correctly.	Notes
_____ _____ _____	

Date

Rewrite the sentence correctly.	Notes
_____ _____ _____	

Vocabulary

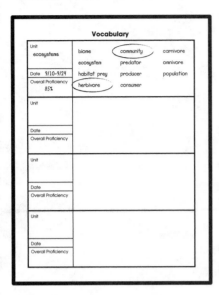

Use this page to track the vocabulary words you teach throughout the year. It is ideal for recording vocabulary introduced through word study, novel study, or science and social studies units. Record the name of the unit or other identifying feature (for example, a book title and/or chapter number) and the date(s) of study. Record the vocabulary words to the right. Assess class mastery and record the proficiency below the date. If desired, circle the words that few students understood for easier reteaching.

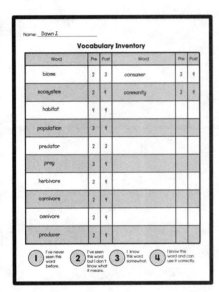

Use this page to allow students to preview and self-assess their understanding of vocabulary words for a unit. Provide the page to students before beginning a unit and preprogram the vocabulary words or have students record them in the spaces provided. Beside each word, students should use the 1–4 scale at the bottom of the page to assess their knowledge of the word. After the unit, have students repeat to see their growth.

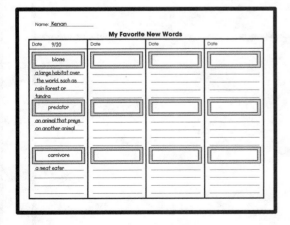

Assess students' individual knowledge of vocabulary with this page. Have students record their favorite new words from a unit and provide a definition or a sentence using the word to prove understanding. You may choose to have students record new words quarterly, or at the end of a unit. Keep this page as a record of learning throughout the year or have students keep it as a personal dictionary.

Vocabulary

Unit	
Date	
Overall Proficiency	

Unit	
Date	
Overall Proficiency	

Unit	
Date	
Overall Proficiency	

Unit	
Date	
Overall Proficiency	

Name: _____

Vocabulary Inventory

Word	Pre	Post	Word	Pre	Post

 1 I've never seen this word before.

 2 I've seen this word but I don't know what it means.

 3 I know this word somewhat.

 4 I know this word and can use it correctly.

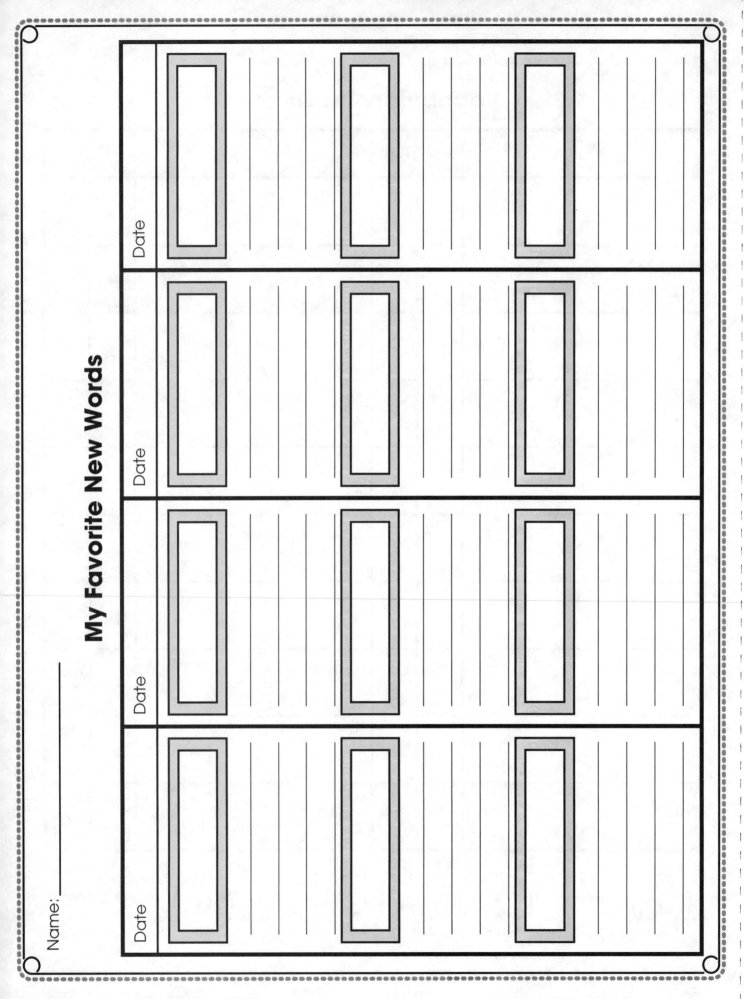

My Favorite New Words

Name: _____

Date

Date

Date

Date

Unknown Words

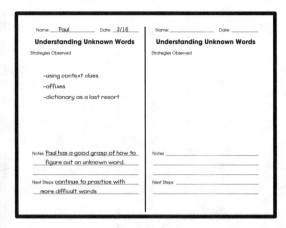

Use this page to assess individual students' mastery of understanding unknown words. Provide the student with several sentences that include unknown words and ask him to define each word. Ask the student to explain how he knew what the word meant. Then, record any strategies you observed and write any additional observations in the *Notes* section. Record next steps, such as ideas for remediation areas, in the bottom section.

This page allows for individual assessment of understanding unknown words. Provide the student with several sentences with an unknown word in each. Have students record and define each unknown word and complete the explanation. Then, students should rate their work in the box at the bottom of each section, using the 1–4 scale provided at the bottom of the page. Use the *Notes* section to record any observations. If desired, divide the page in half and use as a pretest and posttest or as a test and retest.

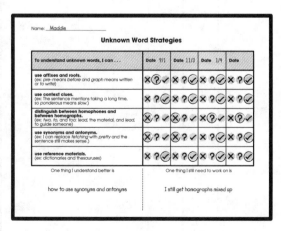

Use this page to help students keep track of their learning during the year. Have students complete the first column by adding the date and circling, coloring, or highlighting the appropriate symbol for each I Can . . . statement. An *X* means *not yet*, a *?* means *maybe*, and a ✔ means *yes*. Have students repeat the self-rating several times throughout the year (such as quarterly) and answer the prompts at the bottom to assess their overall learning.

Understanding Unknown Words

Name: _____ Date: _____

Strategies Observed

Notes _____

Next Steps _____

Understanding Unknown Words

Name: _____ Date: _____

Strategies Observed

Notes _____

Next Steps _____

Unknown Words

I think it means _____

_____

because _____

_____

_____ .

Rate It	Date

I think it means _____

_____

because _____

_____

_____ .

Rate It	Date

I think it means _____

_____

because _____

_____

_____ .

Rate It	Date

I think it means _____

_____

because _____

_____

_____ .

Rate It	Date

Notes _____

_____

1 I don't understand yet.

2 I can determine unknown words with help.

3 I can determine unknown words correctly.

4 I can teach it to others.

Unknown Word Strategies

To understand unknown words, I can . . .	Date	Date	Date	Date
use affixes and roots. (ex: *pre-* means *before* and *graph* means *written* or *to write*)	✗ ? ✓	✗ ? ✓	✗ ? ✓	✗ ? ✓
use context clues. (ex: The sentence mentions taking a long time, so *ponderous* means *slow*.)	✗ ? ✓	✗ ? ✓	✗ ? ✓	✗ ? ✓
distinguish between homophones and between homographs. (ex: *two, to,* and *too*; *lead,* the material, and *lead,* to guide someone)	✗ ? ✓	✗ ? ✓	✗ ? ✓	✗ ? ✓
use synonyms and antonyms. (ex: I can replace *fetching* with *pretty* and the sentence still makes sense.)	✗ ? ✓	✗ ? ✓	✗ ? ✓	✗ ? ✓
use reference materials. (ex: dictionaries and thesauruses)	✗ ? ✓	✗ ? ✓	✗ ? ✓	✗ ? ✓

One thing I understand better is

One thing I still need to work on is

Affixes and Roots

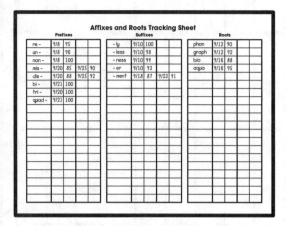

Use this page to track the affixes and root words you teach throughout the year. Record the affix or root and the date it was taught to the right. After assessing class mastery, record the overall proficiency beside the date using a scale of your choosing, such as percentages, check marks, or E/P/M. If needed, reteach the affix or root and record the new date and proficiency level.

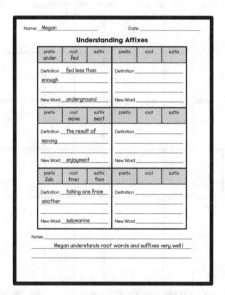

Assess students' individual knowledge of affixes and roots with this page. Prepare index cards with words that include prefixes, suffixes, or both. Have students record the word in the top spaces, breaking it into its parts, and then provide a definition and write a new word using one of the affixes or the root to prove understanding. Use the *Notes* section to record any observations. If desired, divide the page in half and use it as a pretest and posttest or as a test and retest.

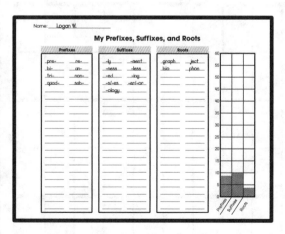

Provide this page to students to allow them to track the affixes and roots they have learned and mastered. As students prove mastery of an affix or root, allow them to record it in the correct section. Periodically, students should count their lists and complete the bar graph on the right-hand side of the page, adding to it as necessary throughout the year.

Affixes and Roots Tracking Sheet

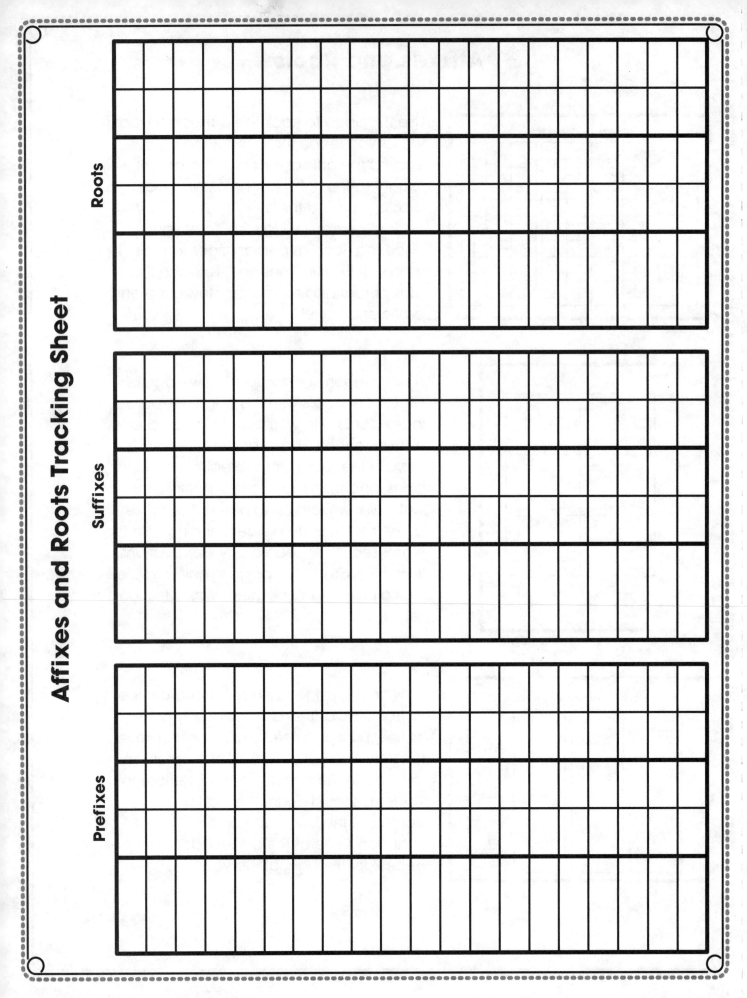

Prefixes

Suffixes

Roots

Understanding Affixes

prefix	root	suffix

Definition _____

_____

_____

New Word _____

prefix	root	suffix

Definition _____

_____

_____

New Word _____

prefix	root	suffix

Definition _____

_____

_____

New Word _____

prefix	root	suffix

Definition _____

_____

_____

New Word _____

prefix	root	suffix

Definition _____

_____

_____

New Word _____

prefix	root	suffix

Definition _____

_____

_____

New Word _____

Notes _____

_____

_____

Name: _____

My Prefixes, Suffixes, and Roots

Prefixes

Suffixes

Roots

60
55
50
45
40
35
30
25
20
15
10
5
0

Prefixes Suffixes Roots